Bridgehampton
Weekends

Bridgehampton Weekends

EASY MENUS FOR CASUAL ENTERTAINING

ELLEN WRIGHT

Photography by Tom Eckerle

WILLIAM MORROW
An Imprint of HarperCollinsPublishers

HarperCollins books may be purchased for educational, business, or sales
promotional use. For information please write: Special Markets Department,
HarperCollins Publishers Inc., 10 East 53rd Street, New York, NY 10022.

FIRST EDITION

Designed by Deborah Kerner

Photography by Tom Eckerle

Printed on acid-free paper

Library of Congress Cataloging-in-Publication Data

Wright, Ellen, 1940–
Bridgehampton weekends : easy menus for casual entertaining /
Ellen Wright ;
photography by Tom Eckerle.
p.   cm.
Includes index.
ISBN 0-688-17091-9
1. Entertaining.   2. Menus.   3. Quick and easy cookery.   I. Title.
TX731 .W733 2000
642—dc21
99–049797

00   01   02   03   04 RRD 10 9 8 7 6 5 4 3 2

In memory of

Mama Wright,

who loved to cook

ACKNOWLEDGMENTS

Joe, my love, my friend

Carla, who believed

Claudia, Alexis, and David, my very wonderful children,
who tested and tasted and loved

Jessica, my niece and friend, without whom I couldn't have done this book,
and her mom, Joyce, who has always been there for me

Carole, whose friendship never flagged

Evie, such help

Bob, for wine advice

Whitmore's Landscaping

Mariann and Grady, who know and show

Tom for beautiful photos, support, etc.

Marcos, help in black

To my testers:

Gerri, Connie, Gladys, Claudia, Lexie, Theresa, Christy, Gillian,
John and Liz and John III, Gerda, Bonnie, and Meg

Noelle and Gerri, for horses

Pam, and all the Morrow people who made my life easier,
Leah, Carrie, and Kate

Thank you all . . .

CONTENTS

WINTER 63

SPRING 125

SUMMER 205

INTRODUCTION

My celebration of wonderful times in Bridgehampton extends year-round, which explains why I have divided the twenty-two menus that follow among the different seasons—summer, fall, winter, and spring. I cook according to how I want to eat; for example, I like comfort foods, such as stews and soups, in winter, and fresh-tasting flavors like cold berry pie when the season offers great berries in late spring.

If there are two words, that describe all the menus in this book, no matter the season, they are "home cooked" and "delicious!" You will find no frills in any of my recipes, no complications. Instead, you have feasible combinations that I have very deliberately kept easy and that have been praised by people I've served them to. Depending upon the recipe, where helpful, I've also included a section called "Ellen's Tips"—insights I've garnered over the years that I think you might like to know: for example, when to freeze something, what the key to a successful recipe is, why it makes sense to do this or that, or how to stay out of trouble and what to do if you do get into trouble. You don't need professional training to cook these recipes well. I believe that simpler is better, casual is good, and home-cooked food is best.

Along the way, you will see from the photographs throughout the pages how I like to serve drinks, set my Easter table, or plan a party on the patio in spring. Because I'm an interior decorator, all these visuals matter to me, but let me quickly add, they do not matter all that much. While I want it to look good and be comfortable when I entertain, I do not want it to look "done." "Done" is not my style but subtle, understated, and easy—these are the words that describe my philosophy. I hope what you see in Tom Eckerle's gorgeous photographs helps to inspire you.

A friend of ours, a Hollywood film director, Mark Rydell, was once asked what it was that he liked so much about coming to dinner at our house. He thought for a minute, then replied that he felt that I really cared and that I wanted him to enjoy his food and to feel at home. He was right. That is why I like to entertain: I want people to feel welcome and taken care of.

If there is one thing I have learned from having lived in many houses over the last thirty-odd years, giving dinner parties and having houseguests wherever we've been, it's to have confidence in the way I entertain. It is just the way I know I would like. The success of a gathering, be it an intimate dinner for two, a fancy dinner party for twelve, or a birthday lunch for my granddaughter turning one, is the sum of its parts. It is not just the food, not just the people, and not just the setting. It is how it all comes together. There are ways to make it work, to make it effortless, and to put people at ease so they can really enjoy themselves and have a good time. And there are ways to make your guests want to come again.

I've been going to the summer resort of Bridgehampton on the south shore of Long Island since 1971, when we first rented a tiny two-bedroom house on Town Line Road for the family, including our three small children. It was a shack, really, but that didn't seem to matter. We could walk to the beach, and we spent the summer eating, laughing, and drinking with friends. We had a wonderful time.

Like so many people who visit Bridgehampton, we were hooked. It became etched in our hearts as a place to have fun, a place for me to entertain family and friends with the cooking I love to do. It is hard not to be charmed. The village of Bridgehampton is beautiful, the ocean is close by, and the fields surrounding it are captivating and peaceful. I had heard people speak of the wonderful memories they had of special summer places that they had gone to over the years, such as Martha's Vineyard, Massachusetts, Dark Harbor, Maine, and Fishers Island, New York. I had wonderful memories myself of a spot where my grandfather used to take my brothers, cousins, and me—a cottage on Samson's

Pond at Cape Cod, in South Carver, Massachusetts. We called it Grandpa's Camp, a camp he loved, where he took us fishing and boating and taught us card games and how to cook the fish we'd just caught over a fire. I will never forget the time when I was about eight years old and I stole the rowboat that was tied up at Grandpa's dock and rowed out to pick water lilies. When he discovered that I was gone, along with the rowboat, he went looking for me, fearing the worst. Instead of punishment, he gave me a big bear hug and suggested I ask him next time. I wanted a wonderful family retreat like that of my own someday. I found it in Bridgehampton.

Bridgehampton has always had a certain kind of magnetism for people. Settled in 1640 by people from Lynn, Massachusetts, Bridgehampton throughout the seventeenth century and most of the eighteenth century was a farming and whaling community. However, if you visit the early-nineteenth-century Corwith House, a museum on Main Street in the village, you will see that as early as the 1870s families were going to Bridgehampton for summer holidays. And not all New York City people either. Bridgehampton was a favorite summer resort at the time for people from all over the United States. A guest registry on the second floor of the Corwith House, which, like many others in the village, was converted to a boardinghouse, shows that in July 1896, families from Ohio and Kentucky came to Bridgehampton for a stay. Marvelous old grainy photographs depict some of the summer visitors back then: the

men in trousers, vests, and jackets, the women in long skirts and hats. Whether they are relaxing on the grass or at the beach (in all those clothes), one thing is clear: They look like they are having a great time.

Nothing has changed about how people like to enjoy themselves when they're in Bridgehampton, although they wear far less straitlaced clothing nowadays. And while much of Bridgehampton has physically changed in the last one hundred and twenty years, the attractions that drew people to the whole East End of Long Island, and more specifically Bridgehampton, remain what they were when those Ohioans and Kentuckians came.

What are they? They are as simple as can be: magnificent land, beautiful sky, the ocean nearby with some of the most spectacu-

lar beaches in the world, and mostly reliable summer weather. The fields of this part of the world, with their famous Long Island potatoes, may be dwindling in number, as are the farmers who once owned those fields, but the meeting of land and sky, with the smell of the ocean, is still the same. The Atlantic Ocean and its border of soft white sand work their magic on you, as only coastline and ocean can. Before you know it, you are spellbound, and that's before you even consider all that the area has to offer from a social and cultural point of view. For me, that has never been the appeal. I am very glad to know that there are museums and galleries and any number of trendy restaurants and sophisticated boutiques nearby. Do I go to them? Not often, but that has less to do with them and more with me.

Once we arrive at our house on

Mitchells Lane from New York City, I don't want to leave. I love the house and the land it is on. Our property is north of the highway, also known as Montauk Highway, or Route 27. Land south of the highway, between Route 27 and the beach, has long been prized real estate in Bridgehampton and in points beyond (East Hampton, Amagansett, and so on). The closer you get to the ocean, the more expensive the land becomes.

When we first started looking for a place to buy in Bridgehampton, there were two things we knew right away: We wanted to be where it was quiet and protected and we wanted a bigger piece of land than we could afford closer to the beach. So it was not surprising at all when we were shown an old farmhouse on an open spacious piece of land north of the highway, with horse farms and fields on either side, that we kept going back for just one more look. I can tell you, it wasn't the condition of the house that sold us. It was in major need of help. Neither my husband, Joe, nor I cared about that; the site was right. It had 360 degrees of sky. It was a bit like being in Montana.

We have redone the house from the ground up, adding on here and there, putting in tall windows to get the most of our wonderful view and stone fireplaces to make everything cozy. We have built a big eat-in kitchen, or "great room," as it is now called, a terrace for outdoor dining, and a small indoor dining room if we need it, although we usually eat in the kitchen where I can cook and talk and see

everything and everyone. Joe loves to garden and so a parcel of land, facing east, was turned over for that.

We now have the perfect setting to do what we love most. As a very young child, maybe four years old, I used to stand by my Russian grandmother, Bessie, my father's mother, in her kitchen in Brookline, as she made special pastries called *bulkis*, sweet rolls that I just adored, on an old kitchen table. It's this warm family cooking tradition that I continue in my kitchen in Bridgehampton.

My own mother was not nearly the cook Bessie was, although she could cook if she wanted to; she did have a handful of recipes—delicious fried onion sandwiches for lunch, an unforgettable chicken cacciatore for dinner, accompanied by dilled cucumbers (the recipe for those are in this book), and a great roast beef seasoned with whole allspice (page 145) that everybody remembers to this day. My mother is a gifted painter and sculptor, an intellectual who always wanted to go back to school. She was the mother of three, and my wonderful father worked long hours at a shoe business he was committed to. Mother did not have the opportunity to pursue many of her interests, so I think she decided that if she couldn't, maybe I could. We took painting classes together when I was six. I learned how to play the piano, taking lessons from age six to eighteen. At nineteen, I went to Mills College in California, where I painted and learned all about ceramics and how to work with clay. It was the pottery, I now realize, that really piqued my interest in cooking. I loved

knowing how things came together and I loved using my hands.

I have never forgotten the first cooking demonstration I ever went to. It was in San Francisco, around 1961. Julia Child was holding a seminar on how to make quiche, which, as a lot of us recall, was *the* dish at the time. As only Julia could, she made the pastry and the filling with incredible ease, and then she put them together and suddenly it was quiche! I remember watching her and thinking about the construction. I can do that, I thought. I knew how to use my hands. I knew about consistency and texture, and I wasn't afraid.

From that moment on, no recipe was too hard for me. The more complicated it was, the better I liked it! The *Gourmet Cookbooks*, volumes I and II, with recipes that were so brief in their instructions that they bordered on vague appealed to my own creativity. They became my bible. Cakes, French pastries, soufflés—you name it, I tried it. I was lucky at the time to have a husband who was himself a good cook and who taught me a lot about spices and seasoning. But there was something I had realized by that time. I was intuitive and brave in the kitchen—in fact, fearless. I always made new things for company and I loved the challenge. I had learned from painting to trust my eye; I had learned from playing the piano to trust my timing. I had a good palate and I knew how to balance amounts, colors, and textures.

That was in the 1960s in California. By 1967, I was the mother of two little girls, divorced and newly remarried to a physician,

BEEBE WINDMILL

Built 1820

who had just been offered a job in New York City in the Lindsay administration. Knowing very few people at all, we set off for New York. People very generously extended themselves to us, and I decided that there was only one way to reciprocate—invite these people for dinner along with other friends. Little by little, we met many new people in various fields. Some of them were in communications and journalism. Some, like our dear friends Tom and Meredith Brokaw, for instance, had also come from California. So my husband wanted to have a big grand dinner, but I knew that was all wrong. I invited them to eat with us in our kitchen, just the four of us, over guinea hen and lentils, and we shared many meals to come.

It was in the early 1970s, though, at a party where, once again, I did not know that many people, that I found myself sitting across the table from James Beard. We were talking about where he bought butter and cheese and the best produce. I think we were both trying to ignore the insurmountably bad catered meal we were served. By the end of the evening, on our way out, I asked him if he would like to come for dinner sometime. He looked shocked and said, "I'd love to, nobody ever wants to cook for me." He did come for dinner not long after that and for many more: We spent many holiday meals together over the years and I even had the pleasure of planning his seventy-fifth birthday party. I took cooking classes with him, worked on developing recipes for his books, and at his behest, brought him home-cooked food when he was in the hospital. (At the time, he also had a stash of champagne in the shower, but that's another story altogether.) He was a great friend, a mentor, and he was always straightforward with me. "It's not the food Ellen cooks," he remarked one time, "that is her strongest suit, although it is good. It's how she puts everything and everyone together and how she makes people feel so at home. That's what she does best." That small bit of James Beard brings me right back to the reason for this book and provides a

big insight into how and why I entertain the way I do. Whether it is a spring dinner on the screened-in porch or a weekend-long house party in the summer, there are certain principles I rely on when it comes to entertaining. I have learned them from experience. I know they work and I want to share them with you.

Number 1: Keep it simple. There is the temptation to want to impress your guests with a dazzling dish at each and every course. I used to tackle it all, from the homemade pastry for the hors d'oeuvres to the crème anglaise for dessert. You don't have to do all that. Unless you are serving real professional cooks and chefs, most of your effort will go unnoticed. Stay focused. Make it easy.

Concentrate all that energy on only one or two dishes so that it really comes out perfectly. It could be only the main course and dessert, or soup. Load the deck in your favor. With fewer complicated dishes to worry about, your chances of success go way up. Also, you'll have more time and energy to enjoy your own party, something many hosts forget.

Number 2: Avoid last-minute panic. There are two distinct ways to do this, only one of which has to do with the preparation of food. First, organize yourself early. Think about who is coming and what you feel like eating. Get a handle on the details of how the meal should look and taste: (1) Know where you are dining; (2) Select the tablecloth, napkins, and decorations you want to use; (3) Be sure you have chosen plates for all the courses; and (4) Order or cut the flowers for the table and house in advance.

Second, when it comes to the food, make what you can in advance. If it is an entire course or even two that can be fully or partially readied ahead of time, do it. I do not believe that every dish must be made the minute before it is served. In a fully staffed kitchen, this works, but at home, it doesn't. Make the hors d'oeuvre, soup, or stew ahead of time, and freeze it. There is no reason not to take advantage of the freezer if you know that the dish can be frozen. Some dishes, of course, cannot. In that case, it is important to plan how you are going to spend your time. Make yourself a schedule if you like.

Number 3: Mix and match. I love the look of dishes, patterns, and glasses that don't all match. As long as you don't go completely haywire, mixing and matching can make for a beautiful table, one with lots of visual interest and excitement. Perfectly matched may be perfect, but, for me, less than perfect is best.

Mix your dishes and patterns and mix the people you invite. I often put together people with completely different interests and backgrounds, from completely different places. It always works. It makes people more interested and a little off balance. I've discovered people tend to be more themselves when they feel relaxed and at home—which is a good place to be! Remember, the more diverse the mix, the better the party.

Number 4: Get guests to help. First of all, it breaks the ice. Second, we all need support, no matter how organized you are. And don't think that a CEO whom you have invited is above pouring wine or passing a plate of hors d'oeuvres.

Number 5: Stay calm. When it comes to the food, what is the worst that can possibly happen? A dish burns beyond recognition and is past the point of salvation? In that event, you do have a problem! But how many times does that ever occur, to even the most inexperienced cooks? Barring that, what's the next worst thing that could go wrong? That a dish won't turn out quite the way you had hoped? Before you go into a complete state of panic, remember that there are things you can do to save the day. More herbs, a quick sauce, some bread crumbs, a different serving dish, a spoon instead of a fork can make all the difference. There is almost always something that can be done. And remember that the more practice you have entertaining, the better at it you will become.

From the macro to the micro, while we're at it, here are a few other things you may want to keep in mind:

Number 1: Keep the cocktail hour short. The reasons are obvious.

Number 2: Do not feel obliged to always make hors d'oeuvres. When I've prepared a menu of three or four courses, I serve very little with the drinks. "There is nothing wrong," James Beard once told me, "with a bowl of black olives as an hors d'oeuvre."

Number 3: A corollary to Number 2: When you are not serving a first course, make an hors d'oeuvre that does not compete with the flavors of the main course. Too many tastes for the tongue is not a good thing. The poor tongue doesn't know what to think! Garlic again! Basil in everything! Less is more.

Also, when serving hors d'oeuvres, whether they are homemade or not, be careful of overdoing it. If the hors d'oeuvres are good, people tend to fill up on them and then the main course goes unnoticed.

Number 4: Avoid flower arrangements that are so tall that they prevent you from seeing the person across the table. I almost always choose arrangements that are no more than 5 or 6 inches in height. In fact, my favorite thing to do is to float flowers in a shallow dish. I never use fragrant flowers on a dining table because the smell interferes with the food.

Number 5: No smoking inside the house. Old-fashioned, perhaps, but I insist.

It took an incredible three days by stage-coach, in the late 1700s, to go from the Fulton Ferry in Brooklyn to Sag Harbor, the famous whaling port on the northern coast of the South Fork. It then took yet another coach or buckboard to get from Sag Harbor to Bridgehampton. Another hundred years would have to pass before the railroad came to this part of the world, in 1870. Those visitors in the marvelous old photos at the Corwith House most probably came to Bridgehampton by train. What a journey that must have been! Now people pour in in every conceivable way—by plane, train, helicopter, car, motor-

cycle, boat, and jitney. Bridgehampton has changed. But there are still glimpses of the Bridgehampton of old—at the Corwith House, at the library, in a visit to the Presbyterian church across the way. Even the lamps at the railroad station bespeak another time. And some things will never change: the beauty of its fields and beaches and sky, the charm of farm stands along a single-lane road that ends with a huge farm, the simplicity of picket fences with climbing roses, the plain loveliness of a shingled house with white trim—the best of Bridgehampton.

FALL

FALL

If Memorial Day weekend is the official start of the summer season in the Hamptons, which it is, then Labor Day weekend is the official end of the summer and start of fall. It has nothing to do with the weather changing. September weather can be every bit as hot as an August, especially at the beginning of the month. I'm talking about the summer exodus that takes place on Labor Day weekend—the long line of cars that starts some time on Labor Day itself and creeps, at a snail's pace, west. For most people, the summer season—whether it's a vacation or a summer rental—is over. It will be almost a whole year before everything revs up again to that fever pitch, and, I confess, that's okay by me. Summer is nonstop and busy, but fall is a great time of the year.

One of the reasons I find fall so appealing is the newfound quiet. There are fewer people and cars and crowds, though it's not like it was in the late 1970s, when some of the stores in the village actually shut down for the winter. There are the pumpkins in the fields, the apples on the trees at several orchards along the way, and the gourds, squashes, and Indian corn you see at the farm stands. Vibrant autumn color dots Bridgehampton, not like in Vermont or other parts of northern New En-

gland, but enough color to accent the simple brown fields and the landscape. It makes me look at everything differently and appeals to my eye. I love it when our row of burning bushes along the driveway turns to vibrant red. No sooner do they turn their brightest, than they begin to disappear.

The air changes, too. The ocean starts to cool off and so do the daytime temperatures, to say nothing of the temperatures at night. We open our windows at night and love the smells and breezes that flow through. You can feel the cool air on your skin when you go into town to the Candy Kitchen for the paper in the morning. (And in fall, unlike in summer, the good news is that there is still a paper left to buy, even if you are a bit late!) As you get in the car, you realize you need a sweater and that is such a nice feeling. That brisk fall air reminds me of growing up outside of Boston, where cold was something you took in stride. I especially like to watch the horses in the fields when it turns really nippy. They frisk and kick around, with a completely different attitude.

Fall foods are also some of the best foods to cook: comforting old standbys like meat loaf and mashed potatoes, flaky old-fashioned apple pie, made with the apples you've just bought from the local orchard, short ribs that bake for 2 hours or more. Like the soups and stews of winter, fall foods fill the house with delicious smells that make you want to come home and relax. Spices like cinnamon and nutmeg are the fall smells that emanate from the kitchen. Dishes that please everyone are the ones I especially want to eat myself.

Because more and more people with homes in the Hamptons use them year-round, getting friends together for lunch or dinner on a fall weekend is easy to do when you feel like entertaining. Fall for my children, on the other hand, is never an easy time for them to visit—school has started and obligations call. One fall weekend we always hope for, in October, is a visit from my brother Myles and his wife, Joyce. Sometimes they drive down from Massachusetts and we always have a wonderful time. Not with all the cajoling in the world have I ever been able to budge them from their house on the Cape in the summer. It's just as well; we have a great time together laughing about old memories, some of which centered on a rather notorious meal that took place in San Francisco, a menu that has come to be called "My Brother Myles's Most Requested Dinner" (page 16).

The one fall day that everyone plans well in advance is Thanksgiving. Nothing interferes with our gathering as a family. Friends are invited, including in-laws, my ex-husband, his wife, his sister, her beau, and his

mother—all at one time! It is really a fun dinner. Given the number of dishes I know how to cook and like to cook, you might find it something of a surprise to learn that the menu for our Thanksgiving dinner hardly ever changes. My children like the one we've had for years, the one they've come to count on.

So I always know what I'm doing Thanksgiving. I make one last trip to the store or farm stand, which will close right after the holiday. Then I'll make the turkey, stuffing, and vegetables, while everyone else brings something to fill in—perhaps an hors d'oeuvre or an extra dessert. It is a real feast, with the tables decorated in autumn colors and a fire roaring in the kitchen. Everyone helps out, which is essential to a family party—even the small grandchildren, who may perform a simple task such as passing the olives.

On the weekends when it is just Joe and me, we might have breakfast at the Candy Kitchen and then go to the antiques show. There are antiques shows in the summer, too, but somehow we have more time in the fall. They are always less crowded and there is always a close place to park—something I have grown to appreciate.

By the first of December, the days are much shorter and the nights are long. It can rain more in December, too, which makes you want to stay home. We build a great fire and we may read or I might make soup or pastry or whatever the spirit moves me to do. The closer it gets to winter, the quieter Bridgehampton

becomes. I can walk leisurely along Main Street and look at the stores that I haven't had time to see.

With the quieter Bridgehampton of fall, I am reminded of the Bridgehampton it once was, without the boutiques and the spe-cialty shops and the upscale stores in the mall. Life was simpler and traveling to Bridgehampton didn't seem like such a chore.

I guess the reason I like fall so much is that you can see that lost part of Bridgehampton best.

Labor Day Dinner for Four

As mad as Memorial Day weekend is, with the traffic and the crowds and the start of summer, so is Labor Day weekend, but in a slightly different way. All the cars are going in the opposite direction this time, back to the city. You can feel the change in the air. Another summer has gone.

My children and their children who have come for the month of August pack up early. It is a long single lane of cars heading west and the sooner they inch into it, the better. Claudia, in particular, has far to go. We say our good-byes: to the swimming, to going to the beach or for ice cream in town after supper, to picking flowers by the side of the road, to the horses in the fields who have become our friends. Then the cars head off down the driveway. It is a bittersweet time.

Too many things are ending.

I purposely ask another couple for dinner that evening—friends who don't have a long drive ahead, who can stay a little longer, until the crush is over. They'll arrive early and we'll have drinks outside and toast the end of another wonderful summer.

Serve this dinner with a light Italian Chianti.

SESAME WAFERS

ELLEN'S TIPS

After baking, be sure to cool the wafers completely before wrapping them well and freezing them in a cookie tin, up to 4 weeks.

Caraway seeds, cumin seeds, black sesame seeds, paprika, and cayenne pepper are a few of the other choices of toppings you can use for these wafers.

These cookies are marvelous with drinks and can be baked ahead, then frozen in a tin. I like to cut them into 3-inch rounds with a biscuit cutter or a juice glass. If I can find a scalloped cookie cutter, I'll use that or perhaps fun cookie cutter shapes, like stars, hearts, or animals. If you freeze them, reheat them after defrosting them, but just briefly. They taste very good warm.

MAKES 30 TO 36 WAFERS

¹⁄₄ cup sesame seeds
³⁄₄ cup all-purpose flour
¹⁄₄ teaspoon baking powder
¹⁄₄ teaspoon salt
3 tablespoons vegetable shortening (do not substitute oil)
3 tablespoons milk
kosher salt for topping

1. Preheat the oven to 350°F.

2. Place the sesame seeds on a cookie sheet and toast until golden brown in the oven, 15 to 20 minutes. Remove from the oven and let cool. Turn off the oven.

3. Sift the flour, baking powder, and salt together in a medium-size bowl. Cut in the shortening with a pastry cutter or two knives until the mixture is mealy. Add the toasted sesame seeds and slowly pour in the milk until the mixture forms a soft ball. Dust the dough lightly with flour and roll out thinly, about ¹⁄₈ inch thick, between two sheets of wax paper. Chill for an hour.

4. Preheat the oven to 325°F. Remove the dough from the refrigerator and peel off the top sheet of wax paper. Cut the sheet of dough into 3-inch rounds with a biscuit or cookie cutter. Put the rounds on a lightly greased cookie sheet leaving 1 inch between each wafer. Bake in the center of the oven, until golden brown, 15 to 20 minutes. Remove from the oven, top with a sprinkling of kosher salt, and let cool on a rack.

MARTINIS WITH SESAME WAFERS

PAN-GRILLED VEAL CHOPS

ELLEN'S TIPS

*The secret to the success
of this dish is pan-grilling
the chops on a hot, dry
cast-iron skillet sprinkled
with coarse salt.*

*Season the chops with the
herbs a few hours ahead of
time for the fullest flavor.*

Crushed rosemary and thyme season these chops—that's all. It's so simple to do that you can't believe how good they are. Be sure the chops are at room temperature before you cook them.

> *1 tablespoon dried crushed rosemary*
> *1 tablespoon dried crushed thyme*
> *four 1- to 1½-inch-thick veal chops*
> *1 tablespoon kosher salt*
> *1 lemon, quartered*

Combine the crushed rosemary and thyme and season the veal chops with about 1 teaspoon of the mixture per chop. Heat a cast-iron skillet or any type of heavy pan over medium-high heat and sprinkle in the coarse salt. Do not add oil. Pan-grill the chops on each side until browned on the outside and slightly pink inside, or to your liking, 8 to 12 minutes per side. Serve with a wedge of lemon.

LIMA BEAN AND
PEA PUREE

This puree always leaves people guessing. They can't quite put their finger on the secret ingredient and, frankly, my advice is not to tell them until they've had a few bites and are asking for more! The dreaded lima bean—how many people do you know who refuse to eat them?—comes into its own here when combined with Le Sueur brand canned peas. This incredible side dish goes beautifully with grilled or roasted meat of any kind as well as poultry.

one 10-ounce package frozen lima beans
    (Fordhook type is best)
one 8-ounce can peas (I like Le Sueur brand),
    not drained
3 tablespoons butter
3 tablespoons sour cream
salt and freshly ground white pepper to taste
4 scallions (green and white parts),
    trimmed, sliced into thin rounds, and chilled

1. Heat the lima beans and peas together in a large saucepan over medium heat until just at the boiling point. Remove from the heat. Drain half the liquid and set it aside. Put the beans, peas, butter, and sour cream in a food processor and process on high speed until smooth. Season with salt and pepper to taste.

2. Place the mixture in a serving dish and cover with aluminum foil. Keep warm. Serve hot and garnish with the cold sliced scallions.

ELLEN'S TIPS

Keep the sliced scallions cold until you garnish at the end. The cold scallions with the hot puree makes for wonderful contrast.

If you like, substitute margarine for the butter and plain yogurt for the sour cream.

BROILED TOMATOES

As a person who paints and decorates, the way a meal looks to me on the plate, the colors and shapes—how it all works together—counts for a lot, and here the red of broiled tomatoes completes the plate and makes the food much more interesting. Usually, I get the tomatoes that morning from our garden. There is really nothing like a ripe homegrown tomato, but vine-ripened ones from the market are an acceptable substitute.

2 medium-size ripe tomatoes
2 tablespoons chopped fresh garlic
2 tablespoons chopped fresh parsley leaves
4 teaspoons extra-virgin olive oil

1. Preheat the broiler and set the rack at close range.

2. Cut out the stem of the tomatoes and cut the tomatoes in half. Set them on a small baking dish cut side up and sprinkle the garlic and parsley on top of each cut half. Drizzle about 1 teaspoon of the olive oil over each tomato half and broil at close range until they are browned at the edges but not wilting, about 1 minute. Keep a close eye on the broiling process so that they are perfectly broiled. Serve immediately.

MUD PIE

ELLEN'S TIPS

Soften your ice cream first so it is easy to spread over the crust.

Make sure the ice cream is set and the fudge sauce is not warm when you pour it on. Otherwise, it doesn't stay on top, it falls into the ice cream.

Serve frozen, but thawed enough to be able to cut into wedges.

There was a wonderful restaurant in San Francisco in 1958 called the Brighton Express, which was run by a short, round Chinese woman married to a tall, thin Englishman. It is the source of this decadent dessert. The Brighton Express was a gourmet restaurant in the late 1950s and 1960s that served quite sophisticated food. This dessert, while really sophisticated but oh-so-very-good, is a godsend, in all sorts of ways. First of all, this recipe makes two pies, one of which you can store in the freezer, all ready to serve whenever you need it. Second, the pies are simple to make. Finally, in just this one dessert are three things most of us love when it comes to treats—Oreos, coffee ice cream, and fudge sauce. What could be better than that?

In 1976, *House & Garden* magazine did a story on my desserts, this being one of the recipes in the article, and my daughter Lexie ended up stealing the show. She was ten years old at the time. I put an apron on her and she helped make this pie. She liked to cook with me back then, and she still does now.

MAKES TWO 9-INCH PIES

For the pies

1 pound Oreo cookies, crushed
1/2 cup (1 stick) unsalted butter, melted
5 to 6 pints coffee ice cream, softened

For the topping

10 ounces semi-sweet chocolate
2 tablespoons butter
1 tablespoon strong brewed coffee (instant is fine)

1. Combine the crushed Oreos and melted butter in a large bowl with a fork. Press the mixture evenly into two 9-inch pie plates.

2. Spread the softened coffee ice cream into the pies over the crusts so that you have at least 1 1/2 inches of ice cream. Place in the freezer.

3. Combine the fudge topping ingredients in a medium-size heavy saucepan. Stir over low heat until completely melted and combined. Remove from the heat and let cool.

4. When the ice cream is really solid (about 3 hours or overnight), pour the fudge topping evenly over each pie. Wrap with plastic wrap and freeze again until the topping is solid. To store them after they are frozen, wrap tightly in plastic wrap and then aluminum foil to keep them fresh.

MUD PIE

My Brother Myles's Most Requested Dinner

CHEESE STRAWS

SESAME SHORT RIBS WITH TORTILLAS

PARSLEYED GREEN BEANS

COLD RADISHES

FRIDAY HARBOR APPLE PIE WITH HOMEMADE
VANILLA ICE CREAM

Serves 6 to 8

My brother Myles, who lives in Boston, has spent the last thirty-plus years summering on Cape Cod and it is near impossible to tear him away from Old Silver Beach in North Falmouth. So we wait for a weekend in the fall when he and Joyce can come to visit.

This is the menu I make when they come. I made this menu for Myles about forty years ago in San Francisco, the night before he was to fly off to Panama to go deep-sea fishing for marlin. We were all very young, and the red wine was flowing. Myles has never been a drinker and he paid dearly for his partying that night and

the next day on the long airplane ride to Panama. I think he wanted to die. We can laugh about it now, but Myles has never forgotten this bittersweet meal.

In fact, it was he who remembered the radishes with the meal.

Serve with cold beer.

CHEESE STRAWS

This is a very rich dough of Cheddar cheese, butter, flour, and egg that bakes up into absolutely incredible sticks or cookie shapes. You can bake them in advance and then when they are completely cool, freeze them. You should reheat them before serving. They are really good served with drinks, as in this menu, or with soup, a salad, or as a snack. They also make a lovely gift at Thanksgiving or Christmas.

MAKES 24 STRAWS

½ cup all-purpose flour
1 teaspoon baking powder
pinch of salt
pinch of Colman's dry mustard
¼ cup (½ stick) butter
⅓ cup grated sharp yellow Cheddar cheese
1 large egg, lightly beaten
2 tablespoons sweet paprika

1. Preheat the oven to 350°F.

2. In a large mixing bowl, sift the flour, baking powder, salt, and dry mustard together. Place the dry ingredients with the butter and cheese into the bowl of a food processor and pulse to make a coarse meal. Add the beaten egg, pulsing until a thick paste forms.

3. Roll out the dough on a lightly floured surface ¼ inch thick and cut into 5-inch-long strips. Sprinkle lightly with the paprika and place them 1 inch apart on a greased cookie sheet. You can twist the strips and press down the ends to make them more interesting. Bake until golden brown, 15 to 20 minutes.

SESAME SHORT RIBS
WITH TORTILLAS

T his is one of the recipes from an old casserole collection, and I can't recommend it enough. The ribs require about 3 hours of cooking, but when they are finished, they are tender beyond belief. The meat falls off the bone. You open up warm corn tortillas and put in the shredded meat, along with the black olives, sesame seeds, and some of the cooking sauce from the ribs. There is something about how it all comes together that is just superb.

1 cup seasoned flour (see Ellen's Tip)
4 large eggs, lightly beaten
4 pounds beef short ribs, trimmed of fat and cut into
*   4- to 5-inch pieces (the butcher can do this*
*   for you, if necessary)*
1 cup sesame seeds
½ cup (1 stick) butter
5 cloves garlic, finely chopped
¾ cup beef broth (canned is fine)
one 8-ounce can tomato puree
1 teaspoon ground cumin
2 tablespoons chili powder
2 dried red chile peppers
5 tablespoons chopped fresh parsley leaves
¼ cup chopped fresh cilantro leaves
1 cup pitted black olives, sliced
1 cup slivered blanched almonds, toasted
twenty-four 6-inch corn tortillas

1. Preheat the oven to 300°F.

2. Place the flour on a plate and the beaten eggs in a shallow bowl. Dredge the ribs in the flour, tapping off any excess, dip in the beaten eggs, and then roll lightly in the sesame seeds to coat completely.

3. Melt 3 to 4 tablespoons of the butter in a large skillet over medium-high heat. Brown the ribs on both sides, in batches if necessary, adding more butter as needed. Remove the ribs to a plate. Add the garlic to the skillet and brown

ELLEN'S TIP

I like to make seasoned flour and keep some on hand stored in a large cookie tin. The recipe is as follows:

2 cups Wondra flour (quick-mixing flour for sauces and gravies)

2 teaspoons garlic salt

2 teaspoons dried oregano

2 teaspoons dried thyme

2 teaspoons dried basil

2 teaspoons freshly ground black pepper

lightly, stirring. Add the broth, tomato puree, and spices and herbs, scraping the browned bits from the bottom of the skillet.

4. Transfer the ribs and broth to a large casserole. Cover and bake, basting frequently, until the meat is very tender, falling off the bone, about 2 hours. Add the olives and almonds and cook 15 minutes more.

5. Butter each tortilla and stack one on top of the other. Wrap them in aluminum foil and keep in a warm oven until ready to serve. Serve the stack of warmed tortillas at the table.

Next spread: **SESAME SHORT RIBS WITH TORTILLAS, PARSLEYED GREEN BEANS, AND COLD RADISHES**

PARSLEYED
GREEN BEANS

The key to cooking vegetables, especially green beans, is not to overcook them. Crisp is key. Use olive oil and lemon juice in place of the butter, if you want. The beans should just glisten.

> *2 quarts water*
> *salt to taste*
> *1½ pounds green beans, ends trimmed and*
>   *cut into pieces or left whole,*
>   *as you prefer*
> *2 tablespoons butter, cut into pieces*
> *2 tablespoons chopped fresh parsley leaves*

Bring the water to a boil in a large saucepan, salt lightly, and drop in the beans. Boil until you can pierce with the point of a knife, 4 to 6 minutes. Drain the water and keep the beans hot in a heatproof serving bowl. Throw the butter on top and cover until you are ready to serve. Sprinkle with the chopped parsley before serving.

VARIATIONS

- Sprinkle with ¼ cup pine nuts or chopped blanched almonds right before serving.
- Cook ⅓ cup minced shallots in 2 tablespoons butter over medium heat until soft and toss with the cooked beans.

ELLEN'S TIP

To keep the string beans green, don't overcook them. Sometimes people cook a vegetable to a point of perfection and then let them sit an hour or more until dinner is ready. During that "sit" time, they overcook. You can undercook vegetables, allowing for this extra time.

COLD RADISHES

If you think cold radishes isn't a recipe, you're right—it's not. But I do want to tell you how I serve them. We're very lucky that over the summer our radishes are homegrown. For the past two years, Joe has been growing a variety of radish that gets as big as a lemon sometimes. They are extraordinarily beautiful, so I put them in a bowl of ice and water and use the bowl as a centerpiece on the table. In the fall, our radish season is over, so I serve them with a bowl of coarse salt for dipping.

ELLEN'S TIP

Leave on some of the green leaves. The radishes look prettier that way.

FRIDAY HARBOR APPLE PIE

ELLEN'S TIPS

Sometimes the edge of the pie will begin to get brown too quickly. If so, take a strip of aluminum foil and press it around the edge of the pie crust to form a "collar." That will prevent the thinner edges from burning.

The cold milk wash and the sugar are what separates this apple pie from most. Most crusts for apple pie are brushed with egg yolk to make a shiny surface. This delicate sugar crust is very good.

My love of entertaining can be traced directly back to my father, who had great style and good taste. For a man who spent a lot of time thinking about and running a shoe business, he also somehow seemed to know exactly how to entertain. I was always amazed as a young girl when he picked out flowers and favors for the going-away lunch for his parents in late fall.

He would have loved being at our table for dinner. My centerpiece for this fall luncheon is a shallow hand-carved wooden bowl filled with perfect Rome apples straight from our neighborhood orchard/stand right on Mitchells Lane. Some of the apples in the basket I buy end up in an apple pie recipe that evolved long ago.

Lynn, who was my roommate at Mills College, came from Friday Harbor, Washington, one of the beautiful San Juan Islands north of Seattle. I was visiting her over Thanksgiving vacation when Lynn's mother made her famous apple pie. The thing that made it unique was her careful way of cutting the apples into paper-thin slices, and arranging them perfectly in the pie. Then she sprinkled sugar on the top crust, which made it extra divine. Alas, she never tasted the dinner, though, because before she could, she excused herself to go upstairs. We suspected it had something to do with too much sherry. I'm sorry she missed her delicious pie.

MAKES ONE 8- OR 9-INCH PIE

> ³/₄ cup granulated sugar
> ¹/₂ teaspoon ground cinnamon
> ¹/₄ teaspoon freshly grated nutmeg
> double recipe Foolproof Pie Crust (page 284)
> 8 Granny Smith or pippin apples, peeled, cored,
>   and sliced ¹/₄ inch thick, about 8 cups
> 3 to 4 tablespoons unsalted butter
> 1 tablespoon cold milk

1. Preheat the oven to 450°F.

2. Combine ¹/₂ cup of the sugar, the cinnamon, and the nutmeg in a little bowl.

3. Roll out half of the dough on a lightly floured work surface to measure ¹/₄ inch thick. Fit it into an ungreased 8- or 9-inch pie plate.

4. Arrange a layer of the apple slices neatly over the dough. Sprinkle the apples with 2 tablespoons of the cinnamon-sugar mixture; dot with 1 tablespoon of the butter. Continue layering, sprinkling, and dotting until the apples are used up.

5. Roll the remaining dough out the same way and place it over the apples without stretching it. Crimp the top and bottom edges together and brush the top with the cold milk. Make four or five 1-inch-long slits in the top for the steam to escape, then sprinkle with the remaining ¼ cup sugar. Place the pie in the center of the oven and bake for 10 minutes. Reduce the oven temperature to 350°F and bake until the pie is light brown and bubbling, about 30 more minutes.

HOMEMADE
VANILLA ICE CREAM

ELLEN'S TIPS

*Using a vanilla bean
makes this ice cream
perfect.*

*Join the hot milk and eggs
slowly and you will not
have any curdling
problem. Don't rush
this process.*

Anyone who has ever tasted real homemade ice cream knows that there is nothing else like it in the world. And vanilla is the standard against which all ice creams can be judged. If it is good vanilla, it's good ice cream. Use a vanilla bean for the best flavor. You will need an ice cream maker, and it is worth investing in one just to be able to enjoy this old-fashioned pleasure. Try the ice cream plain, without any of the variations, and see if it isn't the best vanilla ice cream you've ever tasted, especially when it tops slightly warm Friday Harbor Apple Pie (page 24).

> 2 cups milk
> ¾ cup heavy cream
> 1 vanilla bean, split down the middle,
>   or 3 teaspoons pure vanilla extract
> 3 large egg yolks
> ½ cup plus 1 tablespoon sugar

1. Bring the milk, cream, and vanilla bean to a boil in a medium-size saucepan over medium heat. Remove the pan from the heat, carefully remove the vanilla bean, scrape the brown seeds out of the inside of the hull, and stir them back into the milk mixture. Discard the hull.

2. Beat the yolks and sugar together in a large bowl until the mixture becomes light yellow. Ladle about ½ cup of the hot milk into the yolk mixture and stir well. Stir another ladle of the milk into the yolk mixture and then add the yolk mixture back into the warm milk. Bring to a simmer over medium heat. Remove from the heat. Stir in the vanilla extract at this point if you did not use the vanilla bean. Let cool. Transfer to the ice cream machine and freeze as directed by the manufacturer.

Sunday Breakfast
in Bed

FRESHLY SQUEEZED ORANGE JUICE

PANCAKES TWO WAYS

CRISP BACON

COFFEE

Serves 2

During the summer, the idea of actually having breakfast in bed is not even worth contemplating. But come fall, that's another story.

One of the most perfect places of all in our house for having breakfast in bed is in our guest room, on the second floor, which is really like a private apartment. You come up the stairs to this cozy bedroom covered in old-fashioned rose wallpaper. Even the ceiling is papered. The blankets are red and white, the sheets have red rickrack trim. It's quiet and peaceful and lovely. On a good day, the sun streams in the eaved windows. You feel safe and happy. And, if it's blustery and cold, which it usually is, with clouds moving across the sky, the atmosphere of roses protects you.

I make breakfast in bed for someone in need of a little extra TLC. What a treat it is to eat and then go back to sleep for a few more winks. My oldest daughter, Claudia, once had a terrible cold and I brought her the pancakes that follow as a special treat. She felt better almost immediately. It was the combination of pancakes, sleep, and mother's love.

PANCAKES TWO WAYS

People usually serve one kind of pancake, but I believe that serving two kinds is more fun. These are two versions of pancakes that we all like. The first, the Southern Hill's Stack, comes from my mother-in-law's country club in Tulsa, Oklahoma, where the chef was nice enough to give me the recipe when I asked for it years and years ago. I've been making them ever since. The secret ingredient is buttermilk, but the baking powder and soda help out a lot, making them very fluffy.

The second version is my own creation, made with a pancake mix, a spoonful of sour cream, an egg, and a little vegetable oil. Sour cream, as everybody knows, improves practically anything. Serve them with maple syrup or a thin layer of favorite jam spread on top. I eat mine dipped in plain sugar!

SOUTHERN HILL'S STACK

MAKES EIGHT 3-INCH PANCAKES

1 large egg
⅔ cup buttermilk
1 teaspoon sugar
1 teaspoon baking powder
¼ teaspoon salt
¼ teaspoon baking soda
3 tablespoons all-purpose flour
2 tablespoons butter, melted, for the batter
2 tablespoons butter, for cooking

1. Mix the egg and buttermilk together in a large bowl. Sift the dry ingredients together into a small bowl and mix with the buttermilk mixture. Add the melted butter and mix lightly with a fork. Do not overmix; lumps are okay.

2. Heat a heavy cast-iron skillet over medium-high heat. Lower the heat to medium and melt 1 tablespoon of butter. Drop one small ladle (2 tablespoons) for each pancake. Let the edges get brown and when bubbles form on top turn the pancakes over. Each side will take a few minutes. Remove each cooked pancake to a heatproof plate and keep warm. Repeat with the remaining butter and batter and serve immediately when done.

MAKES TEN 3-INCH PANCAKES

> *1 cup buttermilk pancake mix*
> *1 tablespoon sour cream*
> *1 teaspoon canola oil*
> *1 large egg*
> *¾ to 1 cup whole milk, as needed*
> *1 tablespoon butter, plus more if needed*

1. Combine the mix, sour cream, canola oil, and egg in a large bowl. Add enough milk, little by little, so the batter is the consistency of heavy cream. Mix with a fork and leave some lumps. Don't beat the batter too smoothly.

2. Heat a large cast-iron skillet over high heat. Lower the heat to medium, melt 1 tablespoon butter, and drop 2 tablespoonfuls of the batter onto the skillet for each pancake. Let the edges get brown and when bubbles form on top the pancakes are ready to turn. Add more butter if needed. Remove each cooked pancake to a heatproof plate and keep warm. Repeat with the remaining batter, adding more butter if needed. When they are all done, serve immediately.

PANCAKES TWO WAYS

1910
THE 250TH
ANNIVERSARY
OF THE
SETTLEMENT
OF
BRIDGEHAMPTON

1941 45   1950 53

1660   1776

Post–Pumpkin Patch Halloween TV Dinner

CARROT STICKS, CELERY STICKS, AND CUCUMBER
SPEARS WITH CELERY SALT

OLD-FASHIONED MEAT LOAF WITH MASHED
POTATOES AND GRAVY

SAUTÉED ZUCCHINI

PUMPKIN SWIRL CHEESECAKE

Serves 6

Right on Route 27, on the way to Bridgehampton, there is a huge pumpkin patch farm where you can pick your own pumpkins. It is the perfect October Saturday afternoon outing. We bundle ourselves up—and the grandchildren if we are lucky enough to have them visit—drive over, and roam the rows in search of just the right pumpkins. They must be round with good long stems; they can't have discolorations or dents and they must have a broad enough face to carve on. Mother Nature is rarely that accommodating. We compromise a little and find good enough pumpkins, lug them to the car, maybe with some Indian corn and colorful gourds, then rush home to get to the really fun part. We all carve faces and see whose pumpkin is the scariest. By the time we're done, dusk is approaching and it won't be long before we can put candles in our pumpkins and put them out by the front door to scare off any night visitors.

Then we'll have a comforting, cozy meal. I put out a plate of sliced carrots, celery, and cucumber with a tiny dish of celery salt for dipping. These munchies seem to satisfy everyone's ravenous appetite until I can get the meal on the table. Meat loaf, mashed potatoes, and pumpkin cheesecake is what we love for our version of a TV dinner. Nothing fancy but very popular. This meal is perfect with a bottle of Spanish Rioja.

35

OLD-FASHIONED MEAT LOAF

Old-fashioned here means home cooked, plain and simple and so much in demand. I never have any leftovers when I make this meat loaf. Be sure to serve it with Mashed Potatoes and Gravy (page 39). This is no-frills food at its best. Some things are so obvious—a meat loaf dinner is clearly made for a crisp fall night.

For the loaf

1 pound ground beef
1/2 pound ground veal
1/2 pound ground pork or lamb
1 medium-size onion, chopped or grated
1 large egg
1/2 cup plain dried bread crumbs
3 to 4 tablespoons cold water
2 tablespoons Worcestershire sauce

For the sauce

1/2 cup ketchup
3 tablespoons firmly packed brown sugar (light or dark)
1 tablespoon Worcestershire sauce

1. Preheat the oven to 350°F.

2. Combine the meats in a large mixing bowl. Add the remaining loaf ingredients and press into an 8½ × 4½-inch loaf pan, making a long indentation in the center. Bake for 25 minutes.

3. Meanwhile, prepare the sauce. Place all of the ingredients in a small bowl and mix to combine. Set aside.

4. Pour the sauce over the top of the loaf and continue to bake until the meat loaf is caramelized and mahogany in color, another 20 to 30 minutes. Serve with Hot and Sweet Mustard (page 38).

OLD-FASHIONED MEAT LOAF
WITH MASHED POTATOES AND GRAVY

ELLEN'S TIPS

Use your hands to mix the meats together. It is easier.

For weight-conscious people, you can substitute ground turkey for any of the meats, if you wish.

The secret to this meat loaf is the water because it makes the loaf light and airy. The combination of meats helps to this end as well.

HOT AND
SWEET MUSTARD

I can't even remember when I started to make my own mustard, but I've done it for years and I am never without a jar in the refrigerator. At Christmastime, I multiply the recipe by five or so and put it in pretty apothecary jars with wide plaid ribbon around the tops for gifts. When we lived in Washington, D.C., and Joe was working at the White House, I gave this mustard to President Reagan and Vice President Bush, and they loved it. So did our dear departed friend Mac Baldrige, who was Secretary of Commerce during the early Reagan years. Mac used to put it on scrambled eggs!

MAKES 2 CUPS

one 8-ounce tin Colman's dry mustard
3 large eggs
1 cup cider vinegar
1 cup sugar

Heat all of the ingredients in a heavy-bottomed, medium-size saucepan over medium-low heat; stir constantly with a wooden spoon. When the mixture thickens to the consistency of mayonnaise, about 10 minutes, remove it from the heat. Don't let the mixture become too hot or the eggs will curdle. Let cool to room temperature, then cover with plastic wrap (or a tight-fitting lid) to prevent a skin from forming. Refrigerate.

ELLEN'S TIPS

There are two things to remember when you make mustard: Cook it in a heavy-bottomed pan, preferably an enamelware pan. Adjust the heat to prevent the sugar from burning.

Stir the mustard with a wooden spoon and be careful not to loosen the blackened pieces that might form on the bottom of the pan. They do not look or taste good in the mustard.

This mustard keeps very well in a tightly covered container. I use an apothecary jar with a spring lid. It will keep for several months.

MASHED POTATOES
AND GRAVY

Everybody loves mashed potatoes. If you do, too, this is a recipe you should make. One last thought about mashed potatoes: Use an old-fashioned masher or ricer and good old-fashioned elbow grease. Leave some lumps. But don't overdo it or your potatoes will be gummy. Gravy is essential even if everyone doesn't partake.

> *6 large russet or Idaho potatoes (about 4 pounds)*
> *3 tablespoons butter*
> *6 tablespoons milk*
> *2 tablespoons sour cream*
> *salt and freshly ground white pepper to taste*
> *Gravy for Mashed Potatoes (page 40)*

1. Peel the potatoes and cut into 2-inch pieces. Place in a large saucepan and cover with cold water. Bring the water to a boil over medium-high heat. Reduce the heat to medium, and simmer until the potatoes are tender when pierced with a knife, about 15 minutes. Drain the potatoes and return to the cooking pot. Mash, using a masher, or run the potatoes through a ricer. Stir in the remaining ingredients (except the gravy) and continue to mash until the potatoes are smooth. Taste for seasoning.

2. Serve hot with the gravy.

ELLEN'S TIPS

A food processor will produce gluey-textured mashed potatoes, which is why I use a ricer or a masher. A few lumps are good; otherwise, you might as well use packaged dry potatoes.

If you are not serving the potatoes immediately, place a sheet of buttered wax paper directly on the surface to prevent a skin from forming.

White pepper is key. It has a stronger flavor and is invisible in the potatoes.

Some people like to make a well in the mashed potatoes to hold the gravy. My brother was one who always yelled, "Don't make a well—don't make a well!" Gravy can be passed with a ladle for people to take as much as they want.

GRAVY FOR
MASHED POTATOES

Stash this recipe away because one day it may come in very handy. It specifically addresses how to make gravy when you don't have enough pan drippings from a roasted or baked meat to make gravy. It's easy to do, can be made ahead of time, and keeps in the refrigerator. It should be absolutely lump-free; it's the potatoes that should have the lumps.

MAKES 2 CUPS

- 2 tablespoons butter
- 2 tablespoons Wondra flour (quick-mixing flour for sauces and gravies)
- 1 tablespoon red wine
- 2 cups beef broth (canned is fine)
- 1 teaspoon tomato paste

Melt the butter in a medium-size saucepan over medium heat. Add the flour and mash with a wooden spoon until the mixture is slightly brown. Whisk in the wine and the beef broth a little at a time until the gravy becomes smooth and thick, about 2 minutes. Add the tomato paste and continue to stir as the gravy thickens. If it needs to be a bit thicker, add a teaspoon more flour; if it needs thinning, add a teaspoon more broth.

ELLEN'S TIPS

To serve with chicken, use chicken broth and white wine. To serve with a beef dish, such as meat loaf or roast beef, use beef broth and red wine.

You must trust your own taste for a sauce like this one. In other words, if you like more wine or no wine, you can adjust your gravy accordingly.

Gravy like this can be made ahead and stored in your refrigerator for 3 to 4 days. It saves a lot of time.

SAUTÉED ZUCCHINI

This is a very easy and quick way to cook zucchini that is a little different. It looks pretty on a plate, too. If you need some color, make the cherry tomato variation.

> 6 medium-size zucchini
> 3 tablespoons butter
> ½ pint cherry tomatoes (optional)
> salt and freshly ground white pepper to taste

1. Wash and peel the zucchini and grate them coarsely.

2. Over medium heat in a large skillet, melt the butter and cook the grated zucchini until it begins to wilt, only a few minutes. If you are not using tomatoes, season the zucchini with salt and pepper and serve.

3. If you are using tomatoes, add the tomatoes and cover the skillet until the tomatoes begin to wilt or wrinkle, about 3 minutes. Season with salt and pepper and serve.

PUMPKIN SWIRL CHEESECAKE

ELLEN'S TIPS

Decorate with Halloween theme things such as marzipan pumpkins, witches, black cats, orange kumquats, persimmons, bittersweet berries, leaves, or whatever creative ideas you have.

To cut the cheesecake, use a sharp knife and a spatula to help lift the wedges. A glass of warm water is good to have handy to dip the knife into before cutting each slice. Cheesecake tends to be sticky and doesn't cut smoothly.

We may have been picking gorgeous pumpkins from the fields in which they grew only the day before, but I do not go to the trouble of preparing fresh pumpkin puree for this batter (although I have). I rely on canned pumpkin puree to make it easy. What is the key to baking a smooth, creamy, moist cheesecake like this one? Several factors are important: a low oven (note the 325°F temperature), long mixing at high speed, and ample cooling time. What you're really doing is whipping the batter to make a creamy cheesecake, and all that work pays off!

MAKES ONE 9-INCH CHEESECAKE

For the crust

2¹⁄₄ cups graham cracker crumbs
¹⁄₂ cup (1 stick) unsalted butter, melted

For the filling

four 8-ounce packages cream cheese, softened
1¹⁄₃ cups sugar
¹⁄₂ teaspoon ground cinnamon
¹⁄₂ teaspoon ground ginger
¹⁄₄ teaspoon ground cloves
4 large eggs
¹⁄₄ cup heavy cream
¹⁄₂ cup canned pumpkin puree

1. Preheat the oven to 325°F.

2. To make the crust, combine the graham cracker crumbs with the melted butter in a medium-size bowl. Press the mixture into the bottom of a 9-inch springform pan. Bake the crust for 5 minutes. Remove from the oven and set aside.

3. Place the cream cheese in a large mixing bowl and beat on high speed with an electric mixer for 2 to 3 minutes. In a small bowl, mix the sugar and spices together and add to the cream cheese, blending on medium-high speed for 2 to 3 minutes, until the mixture is smooth and fluffy. *continued*

PUMPKIN SWIRL CHEESECAKE

4. Add the eggs, one at a time, beating well with each addition. Add the heavy cream and mix well.

5. Place the pumpkin puree in a medium-size mixing bowl with 1 cup of the cream cheese mixture. Set aside. Pour the remaining cream cheese mixture into the prepared crust. Spoon 6 large dollops of the pumpkin mixture evenly over the cream cheese mixture. Use the back of the spoon to gently swirl the pumpkin through the batter to form orange streaks. Be careful not to touch the bottom crust.

6. Place the cake in the center of the oven and bake until the cake is set, about 1 hour and 15 minutes. Remove from the oven, let cool slightly, then refrigerate overnight to set.

A Bridgehampton Thanksgiving

CHEESE AND GRAPES

ROAST TURKEY WITH BREAD STUFFING

YAMS AND SUNFLOWER SEEDS

CRANBERRY-ORANGE RELISH

SWEET GARDEN PEAS

PERSIMMON PUDDING WITH HARD SAUCE

Serves 10 to 12

For the very first Thanksgiving in our new house in Bridge-hampton, we had twenty-five guests. Fortunately, numbers don't bother me! I agree with something I once heard James Beard say when a party of his was getting bigger by the phone call: "Oh, fine. They're all coming? The more the better."

One year for Thanksgiving dinner, we had my children, and their children and extended family. Even my ex-husband, his wife, his mother, his sister, and her fiancé came. Everyone brought something—maybe an hors d'oeuvre or a dessert. My children really love the same exact menu year after year. No variations and no substitutions allowed. I make the turkey and stuffing, the vegetables, and the Cranberry-Orange Relish, which always makes me think of James Beard, because I learned some of it from him.

For the number of times I have made this menu, I still love making it. There is something about Thanksgiving that makes it the most wonderful time of the year. The food is glorious, but it is much more. It's the thrill of family gathering around a table, all different generations, some coming from far away, others near, that's so touching to me. There is nothing I like better than to cook and make the house warm and welcoming for family and friends.

I decorate each table differently. One will have gourds and oranges and persimmons as the centerpiece.

45

Another will feature pinecones and brown nuts of all different sizes. At four or five we'll sit down for the feast. Thanksgiving lasts but one short day. Even though it is a lot of work, the smiles on everyone's face—from old faces to brand-new faces—makes it worth every minute of preparation.

Serve this meal with a chilled Zinfandel.

ROAST TURKEY
WITH BREAD STUFFING

Some people worry endlessly about how long to roast a turkey. Unless you are cooking a whopper, 18 to 20 pounds or more, there really is no cause for alarm. I allow 15 minutes per pound at 350°F, stuffed, and 10 minutes per pound for an unstuffed bird. But don't forget to factor in the time needed for making the stuffing, which brings me to another point. After years of experimenting with all different kinds of stuffings—corn bread, plain bread with sausage, French bread with chestnuts (which I peeled myself and then couldn't write a letter or hold a pen afterward—my thumbs were finished), rice with sausage, etc.—I can say with absolute conviction that I prefer to begin with store-bought seasoned bread crumbs and take it from there. This is simple and delicious—moist and divine—even better than the fanciest ones around.

For the flavored butter

½ cup (1 stick) butter
2 tablespoons prepared mustard (I like Dijon)
2 tablespoons Worcestershire sauce

For the bird

one 10- to 12-pound turkey
2 tablespoons kosher salt

For the stuffing

½ cup (1 stick) butter, melted
1 cup chopped onions
½ cup chopped celery
2 cups corn bread stuffing crumbs
2 cups plain stuffing crumbs
1 cup boiling water

continued

ROAST TURKEY WITH BREAD STUFFING, YAMS AND SUNFLOWER SEEDS,
CRANBERRY-ORANGE RELISH, AND SWEET GARDEN PEAS

Previous spread: CHEESE AND GRAPES

3 cups chicken broth (canned is fine)
2 tablespoons Wondra flour
(quick-mixing flour for sauces and gravies)

I recommend you allow plenty of time for your turkey. It can sit out at room temperature after it is roasted for 20 to 30 minutes with a sheet of aluminum foil covering it loosely before carving.

I like to use Wondra flour for the gravy because it thickens without lumps.

Optional additions to the stuffing may include:

½ cup chopped walnuts
1 cup browned crumbled sausage meat, either breakfast sausage, Italian sweet sausage, or hot sausage
½ cup crumbled canned chestnuts, drained
½ cup chopped, peeled apples
½ cup pine nuts
½ cup golden raisins

1. Preheat the oven to 400°F.

2. To make the flavored butter, melt the butter in a small saucepan. Add the mustard and Worcestershire and stir until well blended. Set aside.

3. Wash the turkey and pat the outside and inside of the bird dry with paper towels. Set aside to prepare the stuffing.

4. Place 2 tablespoons of the melted butter in a large skillet over medium heat and cook the onions and celery until they are opaque. Transfer them to a bowl and set aside.

5. In a large mixing bowl, combine the corn bread crumbs, plain crumbs, and cooked onions and celery together. Add the remaining 6 tablespoons melted butter and the water and toss the ingredients lightly with a fork.

6. Stuff the turkey completely, but not too tightly, and skewer shut the openings. You can stuff the neck end of the turkey. Take the remaining stuffing mix, if there is any, and fill an 8-inch square glass baking dish with the stuffing. Bake for 30 minutes.

7. Sprinkle the skin of the turkey with the kosher salt. Put the turkey on a rack set in a large roasting pan and roast, uncovered, for 30 minutes. Reduce the oven temperature to 350°F and continue baking. Baste the turkey every 30 minutes with the flavored butter until the leg moves freely and the juices flow clear (not pink) when pierced in the joint, about 2 hours or more. Remove from the oven and let rest for 20 minutes before carving.

8. To make the gravy, remove the rack with the turkey and put the roasting pan over medium-high heat. Add half the chicken broth to deglaze the pan, scraping the brown bits off the bottom with a wooden spoon. Add the remaining chicken broth and the flour and whisk until thickened. Strain through a fine strainer and keep warm in a saucepan. Serve piping hot in a gravy boat.

Yams and
Sunflower Seeds

ELLEN'S TIPS

You can do steps two through four up to 2 days before the dinner.

In the morning, pick up with step five and the rest will go like silk.

You can scatter or cover completely with marshmallows, depending on your preference.

Every year, come fall, one of my dearest friends in Chicago, Soni, calls me for this recipe. It means Thanksgiving is here. She always loses her recipes. I immediately fax it to her, knowing full well that next year will be the same. We have these delicious marshmallow-topped yams every year without fail.

½ pound dried apricots, quartered
½ cup sweet vermouth
two 28-ounce cans yams, drained
¾ cup (1½ sticks) butter
juice of 2 limes, about 3 to 4 tablespoons
2 tablespoons firmly packed dark brown sugar
2 tablespoons pure maple syrup
½ teaspoon salt
½ teaspoon freshly ground white pepper
½ teaspoon ground cinnamon
½ teaspoon freshly grated nutmeg
½ pound shelled sunflower seeds
2 large eggs
2 dozen large marshmallows

1. Preheat the oven to 350°F.

2. Soak the apricots in a covered jar with the vermouth at least 3 hours or overnight. Drain.

3. Mash the yams in a large bowl. Add ¾ stick (6 tablespoons) of melted butter, the lime juice, brown sugar, and maple syrup and mix with a fork. Stir in the seasonings and spices. At this point you can refrigerate the mixture, covered well in plastic wrap, overnight.

4. Melt 2 tablespoons of the butter in a medium-size skillet over medium heat. Add the sunflower seeds and cook, stirring, until lightly browned. Let cool, drain on paper towels, and store in a jar. (If assembling the entire yam dish at once, add to the yam mixture.) The sunflower seeds can be stored in the refrigerator, tightly covered, up to 3 days.

5. A few hours before serving, let the yams come to room temperature, if necessary. Lightly beat the eggs and add to the yams, along with the drained apricots and the sautéed sunflower seeds. Combine lightly with a fork. Do not mash.

6. Butter a shallow ovenproof casserole or Pyrex dish with 2 tablespoons of softened butter. Spoon in the yam mixture and lightly smooth over. Arrange the marshmallows on top and dot with the remaining 2 tablespoons of butter. Bake in the center of the oven until the marshmallows are browned, about 30 minutes.

CRANBERRY-ORANGE RELISH

ELLEN'S TIPS

When cranberries come into season, buy several bags and make some relish. It keeps for months on end in the refrigerator, and there is no substitute for fresh cranberries. I have tried this using canned whole cranberries with forgettable results.

Don't think you can substitute fresh ginger for candied ginger; it doesn't work here.

It wouldn't be Thanksgiving dinner in our house without this relish. I like it at other times, too, even with fish! It also makes a late-night turkey sandwich complete.

> *³/₄ cup water*
> *1 ¹/₂ cups sugar*
> *2 cups fresh cranberries, picked over for stems and washed*
> *2 oranges, seeded and cut into 2-inch chunks, peel included*
> *2 tablespoons minced candied ginger*
> *¹/₄ teaspoon ground cloves*
> *¹/₄ teaspoon ground cinnamon*

1. Bring the water to a boil in a large saucepan, add the sugar, and stir to dissolve. Reduce the heat to medium, simmer for 5 to 7 minutes, and let cool. (You can cool this quickly in the freezer for 10 minutes if you are in a rush.)

2. Combine the cranberries and the cut-up oranges in a food processor and chop coarsely. Add the candied ginger, cloves, and cinnamon, and stir the whole mixture into the sugar syrup. Store in the refrigerator at least overnight, until ready to serve.

CRANBERRY-ORANGE RELISH

SWEET
GARDEN PEAS

Every Thanksgiving table needs a green vegetable, and in our house, sweet green peas get the vote. If in the chaos of getting the meal on the table you can remember to sprinkle them with a chopped fresh herb, like mint, thyme, or parsley, they will be that much better.

1 cup chicken broth (canned is fine)
two 10-ounce packages frozen peas or
3 cups fresh peas
1 tablespoon unsalted butter, softened

1. Heat the chicken broth in a large saucepan over medium heat. Drop in the peas and simmer until just barely tender.

2. Drain and cover to keep warm.

3. Add the butter, stir to melt, and serve immediately.

PERSIMMON PUDDING
WITH HARD SAUCE

ELLEN'S TIPS

The hard sauce can be made well in advance and kept refrigerated.

You can heat up the pudding the same way you cooked it. Simmer about 10 minutes for a room-temperature mold, 30 minutes for a cold mold.

I like to use persimmons in salads and they should be ripe, but not mushy-ripe, as they need to be for the pudding. Try them sometime.

A pudding mold with a fitted lid is sold at a kitchenware or hardware store. If you don't have one, you can butter a large piece of aluminum foil and place it butter side down over the pudding in a bowl or dish, tightly fitted. It's best to tie a buttered string around the mold and foil to keep the foil in place while steaming.

An old-fashioned steamed pudding may not be your traditional Thanksgiving Day dessert, but it is a tradition on our Thanksgiving table. You will need a pudding mold and persimmons, a beautiful orange fruit that looks like an apple. The persimmons will need to be quite soft, almost overripe to the touch. Persimmons taste like a cross between a peach and an apricot, but they are a little tart. The pudding should be served slightly warm, which makes the hard sauce—one of the best tastes—melt.

If persimmons are difficult to find or still too hard to use, I can recommend some far more traditional desserts that everybody recognizes and loves: Friday Harbor Apple Pie (page 24), or even Homemade Vanilla Ice Cream (page 26). Or, why not just make both? In this case, the more the better!

For the pudding

½ cup (1 stick) unsalted butter, softened, plus extra for the pudding mold

1 cup sugar

1 cup sifted all-purpose flour

1 cup persimmon pulp (from 2 to 3 ripe persimmons, peeled and seeded)

3 teaspoons brandy

2 large eggs, slightly beaten

2 teaspoons baking soda mixed with 2 teaspoons warm water

½ teaspoon pure vanilla extract

½ teaspoon ground cinnamon

1 teaspoon ground ginger

1 teaspoon ground cloves

½ cup chopped walnuts

1 cup golden raisins

For the hard sauce

½ cup (1 stick) unsalted butter, softened

1 cup confectioners' sugar

1 tablespoon brandy

1. To make the pudding, in a large bowl, cream together the butter and sugar with an electric mixer at medium speed. Add the flour, ½ cup at a time, alternating with the persimmon pulp, brandy, eggs, and baking soda mixture. Stir in the vanilla, spices, walnuts, and raisins and mix on low until the butter comes together, about 5 minutes.

2. Butter the top and bottom of a 2-quart pudding mold with a lid (see Ellen's Tips). Spoon in the mixture. Put the buttered lid on tightly and lock into place. Put the mold in a bigger pot filled with water to come halfway up the side of the mold; cover the pot. It is necessary to have a well-buttered mold and enough water for ample steam for this pudding to come out right. Bring the water to a simmer and let simmer over medium-low heat for about 2 hours. Make sure the water doesn't evaporate; add more hot water if it does. The pudding should be checked with a cake tester. When the tester comes out clean, the pudding is done. Take it mold out of the water and unmold when cool, 1 to 2 hours.

3. While the pudding is steaming, prepare the hard sauce. Cream the butter and sugar together with an electric mixer. Beat in the brandy. Chill at least 1 hour. Serve with the warm pudding.

ELLEN'S TIPS

In England it is common to tie a buttered cloth around the top of a deep, buttered bowl to steam a pudding.

WINTER

WINTER

When you spend both summer and winter weekends in Bridgehampton you really come full circle. Summer has so much going on: one event after another, lots of houseguests, many dinner parties, if you choose to go, and even a few picnics to put together.

Fall arrives—when we are all ready for a change of pace—and we regroup. Fall weekends can be hectic, too, but they tend to be busy in a completely different way: Even though the summer season is over, not everything comes to a stop. And fall weather can be really gorgeous, with long outings for apple and pumpkin picking or walks on the beach. I think of fall as a chance to recharge my batteries and gain some new energy. It reminds me of all that has passed and at the same time provides a taste of what's to come. Fall seems to quietly welcome winter and the settling in.

Come that first weekend in December, you can't help but notice the quiet. You see it, you feel it, and you hear it. Bridgehampton grows still in winter in a peaceful and pleasant way.

The trees are bare by now, and the winds really howl at our house in particular. Outside, four or five horses, each blanketed up, run around in the fields. Winter makes them

look ever more beautiful. A gaggle of Canadian geese has parked themselves in the middle of another paddock. They seem to like to winter in Bridgehampton, too!

Our Bridgehampton routine varies little from what it is in summer. Depending upon the weather, we drive out from New York City either Friday night or early Saturday morning. Unlike in summer when the first thing Joe does when we arrive is check his garden, now he gets ready to warm up the house. He lights a fire in both the kitchen and the bedroom, which are at opposite ends of the house. Almost instantly, the chill disappears.

I put away the food and start to cook—a soup or stew or a pie or biscuits. It will be some version of real winter food, the stick-to-the-ribs kind that nourishes and nurtures and warms the body. If we're having friends for dinner on Saturday night, I may have even made the stew in the city and brought it out with us. Stews and soups always taste better when they are made in advance. If that's the case, then I'll bake some kind of yummy dessert—Susan's Bourbon Cake (page 101) or Russian Blintzes with Sour Cream and Black Cherry Preserves (page 78) just in case we need a sweet dessert.

The house will fill with wonderful

aromas and the windows will fog up a little. And if it then begins to snow—which it does in Bridgehampton, despite it being so close to the ocean—we consider ourselves the luckiest people on earth. For all the years we have been going to Bridgehampton, we have been snowed in only once, and I mean really marooned. When it snows like that, you can hardly see out the window at times. It can snow for hours and it is a very cozy feeling. I remember sitting by the fire looking out at the snow-covered paddock and loving it, enjoying every minute.

So winter is for nesting and taking in the view, but our family has also spent many a Christmas in Bridgehampton. We've never been really snowed in for the big day, but we've had dustings on Christmas Eve maybe a few times over the years. Nothing could be prettier. We leave the city in time to buy our tree at a stand near the high school in the village, take it home, and like everyone else, try to get it to stand up straight. This feat is easier said than done. It's never without an argument, though! Then, my son, David, if he is home, starts to decorate the tree—a tradition that was established by his older sisters, who decided that their brother should not only oversee the job but also undertake it!

Christmas is a really happy time for me, all wrapped up in wonderful memories of my childhood, and especially of a dinner my father used to give on Christmas Day for our entire family. He always held it at the Copley Plaza

Hotel in Boston, in a private dining room, with musicians and presents, mistletoe, and the most marvelous food. It was a glorious party, and it is just that atmosphere I try to re-create at our Christmas dinners.

You can't speak of the holidays at the end of the year, of course, without mentioning the dreaded New Year's Eve! It is a night that I basically could do without and I am happy to report that Joe agrees with me. The only way we like to celebrate it is over an intimate dinner with good friends or family who also happen to be like-minded on the subject, drinking special champagne and eating caviar and good food, with an early witching hour, hopefully before the clock strikes twelve. Frankly, there is no better way to usher in a new year, and I especially recommend the menu for New Year's Eve Dinner (page 103) as a way to start.

Which brings me back to the foods and feelings of winter. Whether you are seated at a damask-covered table sipping Dom Pérignon from crystal flutes or eating on TV trays in front of a roaring fire, certain principles invariably apply. The food, fancy or plain, should obviously be terrific. Some of the most humble meals are the ones people tend to like the best. It's not the dazzling beef Wellington or the puff pastry or the pâté de foie gras, but the Chicken Paprikash (page 97) that people want. Or it's the Beef Bourguignonne (page 85). Or it's the Lamb Shanks with White Beans (page 116). What do they all have in common? For one, they are all made in one pot, a sure sign of home cooking. Second, they are all delicious and have gravy. Finally, each goes with something like mashed potatoes, rice, or hot crusty bread—comfort foods.

In our kitchen in New York City and in Bridgehampton, we have a table big enough for six or eight people to sit at comfortably. Neither table is particularly fancy and in both places the kitchen equipment is right there, in full view. I can't tell you the number of times that people, and some fancy ones at that, have asked me if they can come for supper in the kitchen. Notice the language. It's not "have dinner together"; it is "supper in the kitchen." Home-cooked food around a pretty table in a kitchen may not be right for every occasion, but it has great universal appeal. Try it, in winter.

Easy Sunday Supper

ONION PUFFS

MAMA'S SPLIT PEA SOUP

BLACK PUMPERNICKEL BREAD WITH
SWEET BUTTER

WATERCRESS SALAD WITH ELLEN'S DRESSING

RUSSIAN BLINTZES WITH SOUR CREAM AND
BLACK CHERRY PRESERVES

Serves 6

This one of my favorite Sunday suppers. Depending upon the weather, we try to have dinner in Bridgehampton on Sundays in the winter; even if it's an illusion, it makes the weekend feel so much longer.

Without a doubt, Mama's Split Pea Soup (page 71) is one of the best soups I have ever tasted. You will need a meaty ham bone to make it the way she would want you to, so factor that somewhere into your shopping agenda beforehand. And you must serve the soup with the best pumpernickel bread you can find and sweet fresh butter. The dessert recipe for the blintzes came to me from another grandmother, who came to this country from Russia. A really good cook, she taught me the trick of making great blintzes: Don't make them too big. Three or four small ones are better than two big ones. She was right. And here is something I've learned— don't stint on the sour cream, or the black cherry preserves, either. If you really want to start a day off in great style, serve the blintzes for breakfast.

There's something else about this menu. It doesn't have to do with food, though it explains why I love this menu so. What you have here, wrapped up in this simple meal, are memories—of mothers and grandmothers and of times gone by. That's what is so good about sharing recipes.

Serve with a cold Pouilly-Fumé or a dry, cold Chablis.

ONION PUFFS

ELLEN'S TIPS

You can add some chopped fresh parsley on top of the puffs after broiling.

You can spread some of my Hot and Sweet Mustard (page 38) on top of the onion before the mayonnaise for a spicier version of this recipe.

This is one of my favorite hors d'oeuvres. Normally I make them as rounds, but I have learned that you can also make them larger in sandwich form, which works very well. Any way, shape, or form, these simple toasts are the best. The onions and mayonnaise melt together under the high heat of the broiler and taste delicious. They're a great nibble to serve to get your appetite going, and they couldn't be easier to put together. I like to use a sweet Vidalia onion if I can find it in winter.

> *5 slices sandwich bread (Pepperidge Farm*
> *white bread is best)*
> *mayonnaise as needed*
> *1 small Vidalia or sweet onion, thinly sliced*

1. Preheat the broiler.
2. Toast the bread lightly in a toaster oven. Remove the crusts. Cut the slices with a 2-inch round biscuit cutter and spread the rounds lightly with mayonnaise. Put a slice of onion on top of each piece and spread with mayonnaise again. Broil until golden brown. Serve hot.

MAMA'S SPLIT PEA SOUP

My mother-in-law, Joe's mother, was born in Czechoslovakia, and she had great instincts and knowledge when it came to cooking. She had the gift of common sense, which I think is a real talent in the kitchen. This soup demonstrates her good taste. In the winter I always have a container or two of it in the freezer, ready for thawing. While Mama never insisted on sautéed croutons on top, she would have approved. Joe used to go and visit his mom in Tulsa and even in his fifties she always made him some of this favorite soup for her "boychick."

ELLEN'S TIPS

The recipe needs no salt because the ham bone has enough.

In this recipe you do not need to soak the peas overnight.

I like to use whole-grain bread for croutons. You may also use Italian, French, or sourdough as well.

I sometimes serve grilled knockwurst and my Hot and Sweet Mustard (page 38) with this soup if a more substantial meal is in order.

Ham bones come in different sizes, but the most important requirement is that there be meat on the bone. The bone with the meat will weigh from ½ to ¾ pound.

For the soup

1 ham bone, with meat left on (see Ellen's Tips)
one 10-ounce bag dried yellow or green split peas
   (Mama liked yellow)
1½ quarts cold water
2 medium-size carrots, diced
2 ribs celery, trimmed and diced
4 medium-size onions, thinly sliced
1 bay leaf
1 clove garlic, crushed
1 teaspoon sugar
freshly ground black pepper to taste
2 tablespoons flour
2 tablespoons butter

For the croutons

8 medium-thick slices bread (any type is fine)
6 tablespoons (¾ stick) butter
1 teaspoon vegetable oil

2 tablespoons chopped fresh parsley leaves

1. Place the ham bone in a large stockpot and cover with cold water. Bring to a boil over high heat. Reduce the heat to medium-low and simmer, uncovered,

MAMA'S SPLIT PEA SOUP

for 30 minutes. Transfer the ham bone to a plate and set aside. Discard the water.

2. Rinse the peas in cold water and pick over for any pebbles. Let the peas soak in water to cover for 3 minutes. Drain. Place the peas in a large stockpot and cover with the cold water. Add the ham bone and the remaining soup ingredients except the pepper. Bring to a boil over high heat. Reduce the heat to low and simmer, covered, for 2 hours, skimming any scum off the top as necessary. Stir occasionally with a wooden spoon. Strain the solids and set aside the cooking liquid. Remove the ham bone, carefully pick off the meat into bite-size pieces, and place in a medium-size bowl. Set aside. Discard the bone, bay leaf and any gristle.

3. Make a "roux" by heating the butter in a small skillet over medium heat. Add the flour and stir until it browns slightly. Add the mixture to the soup and mix it in over low heat. Run the peas through a food mill until smooth, or process in a food processor until smooth, 20 to 30 seconds. Add a ladle of cooking liquid to the soup if it is too thick. Place the soup in big saucepan or tureen and return the meat to the soup. Season with the pepper. Keep warm until serving.

4. To make the croutons, take the slices of bread and cut off the crusts. Cut the slices into 1-inch squares. Heat a large skillet over medium-high heat. Add 2 tablespoons of the butter and the oil. Cook the bread until brown on both sides, shaking the pan as the bread cooks. Add more butter as needed. Transfer the croutons to a paper towel to drain, sprinkle the soup with parsley, and serve the croutons alongside in a pretty bowl.

BLACK PUMPERNICKEL BREAD
WITH SWEET BUTTER

No, this is not a recipe, but it is an intrinsic part of this soup supper. Use really good pumpernickel bread and slightly softened sweet butter. There is something delicious about buttered black bread with split pea soup—they were meant for each other.

> *1 loaf fresh pumpernickel bread*
> *1/4 cup (1/2 stick) butter, at room temperature*

Cut the pumpernickel into 1/2-inch-thick slices. Place the sliced bread in a basket lined with a clean napkin or dish towel. Put the butter out in a pretty ramekin.

ELLEN'S TIP

Use pumpernickel with or without raisins and nuts. I prefer without.

WATERCRESS SALAD
WITH ELLEN'S DRESSING

If you can't find watercress, arugula and/or endive would be a good substitute. The point of this salad, or any other salad you may prefer to make with this menu, is to have something cold and crisp to go along with the soup.

> *2 bunches watercress*
> *1 Belgian endive*
> *2 scallions*
> *½ cup Ellen's Dressing (page 232)*

1. Wash the watercress and trim off the large stems. Spin-dry the leaves and add to a large salad bowl. Wash and core the endive and separate the leaves. Cut them into quarters and add to the salad bowl. Clean, pat, or spin the leaves dry. Slice the scallions and add the white and green rounds to the bowl. Cover the bowl with a clean dish towel and refrigerate no more than 2 hours.

2. Toss with the dressing just before serving.

RUSSIAN BLINTZES
WITH SOUR CREAM AND
BLACK CHERRY PRESERVES

Blintzes are very thin pancakes or crepes stuffed with a sweet cheese mixture, which most people only have when they go out, believing they are too hard to cook at home. But they aren't difficult at all, and this is a good recipe to follow—a great place to start your blintz-making career. Blintzes, the pancakes themselves, can be frozen. So go ahead, or as one grandma said to my friend Beth Burstein when she taught her to make them, "Try it. You'll love them."

For the filling

one 16-ounce container cottage cheese, drained
1/2 pound farmer cheese
1/4 teaspoon salt
1/4 teaspoon sugar
1/4 teaspoon ground cinnamon
1 large egg, lightly beaten

For the crepes

3 large eggs, well beaten
1 1/2 cups water
2 cups all-purpose flour
pinch of salt
3 tablespoons unsalted butter
2 cups sour cream
one 8-ounce jar whole black cherry preserves

1. Make the filling: Mash the cottage cheese and farmer cheese together in a medium-size bowl with a fork. Mix in the salt, sugar, cinnamon, and egg. Set aside.

2. To make the crepes, place the eggs in a medium-size bowl and stir well with a fork. Add the water, flour, and salt alternately, and mix until smooth. The batter can also be made in a blender or food processor and quickly pulsed until smooth. It should pour like heavy cream. Add a bit more water or flour to get this consistency.

ELLEN'S TIPS

Making crepes is one of those things where practice makes perfect, so give it some time to get it right.

Sometimes it is fun to serve an assortment of jams: strawberry, raspberry, apricot, and blueberry to name a few. Having said that, a good black cherry preserve is my favorite.

3. Heat an 8-inch frying pan, or a crepe pan, over medium heat. Grease the pan with 1 teaspoon of the butter and add 3 tablespoons of the batter. Tilt the pan until the batter spreads evenly around the pan. When the crepe begins to brown slightly around the edges and becomes dry, turn the crepe out onto a paper towel. You will only cook one side. Repeat with all but 1 tablespoon of the remaining butter and all of the remaining batter until all the crepes have been made.

4. Place 1 tablespoon of the cheese mixture in the center of the browned side of the crepe and fold like a package, turning each flap over the filling and tucking in the edges, so that the filling will stay inside when you cook it. The package should be the size of a small to average-size lemon. Place the blintzes in a row on a pan lined with wax paper, layering with wax paper in between each row. Cover the blintzes tightly with plastic wrap and chill for at least 1 hour before cooking them. At this point the blintzes can also be frozen. They will keep in the freezer for up to 2 months if wrapped well.

5. To serve: Heat the remaining tablespoon of butter in a medium-size skillet over medium heat until it coats the bottom of the pan and is bubbling. Cook the blintzes on both sides until nicely browned, about 4 minutes on each side. Serve immediately with sour cream and black cherry preserves.

Christmas Dinner
by the Fire

PEARS AND WARM BRIE

BEEF BOURGUIGNONNE

KEVEN'S PILAF

MIXED GREENS WITH CHERRY TOMATOES

ANGEL FOOD CAKE WITH SLICED PEARS,
CRÈME ANGLAISE, AND FRESH NUTMEG

Serves 6 to 8

This is the dinner that some of my friends ask to eat with us in the kitchen when they want to relax. An old friend of mine, whom I have known since I was a child and played dolls with in Boston, where we both grew up, loves to come to my kitchen and have this meal.

Our Christmas tree decorator has always been my son, David, if he's home. He's had lots of practice, which started with the disappearance of his older sisters just when the ornament box appeared and needed to be unwrapped, and the lights needed unraveling. David always strung the lights and got the ladder to place the little angel on top of the tree, jobs that nobody wanted. I am happy to report that there were some years when everyone helped and we had a tree-trimming party to celebrate the festivities.

We buy our tree in Bridge-hampton, at the high school, always, it seems, on a day that is bitter cold. Somehow we get it home and put it up in the living room.

What we like to do at dessert time is have our Angel Food Cake (page 91) and coffee in the living room by the tree and in front of a roaring fire.

Serve this dinner with a hearty Burgundy.

PEARS
AND WARM BRIE

This dish is so easy and so special. I peel the pears and slice them, making sure to squirt a little lemon juice over them to keep them white. Then I put the wheel of brie in the microwave (or oven) for about 30 seconds to get the center warm. I remove the cheese from the oven but I don't cut it until everyone is ready for their hors d'oeuvre with their drinks. I serve this with thinly cut French bread slices in a basket with a pretty napkin and put the Brie on a board or plate surrounded by the pears.

BEEF BOURGUIGNONNE

This lovely stew is perfect for winter and it came from a cookbook I used in 1960, which was my bible when I was first learning how to cook. It is French in feeling, and the better the Burgundy you use in it, the better the flavor will be. Like all stews, it is tastier the day after you make it. It makes a lot of servings, which is a bonus because it freezes beautifully. Don't be put off by the number of ingredients, it is not as much work as it appears to be.

4 pounds chuck beef, trimmed of fat and cut
  into 2-inch cubes
½ cup all-purpose flour
¼ cup olive oil
½ cup (1 stick) unsalted butter
freshly ground black pepper to taste
¼ cup cognac, warmed
½ pound thickly sliced lean bacon, cut into 2-inch pieces
4 cloves garlic, crushed and finely chopped
2 medium-size carrots, diced
2 leeks, white part only, cleaned (see Ellen's Tips, page 88)
  and finely chopped
4 medium-size onions, finely chopped
2 tablespoons chopped fresh parsley leaves
¾ cup good quality red Burgundy wine
bouquet garni (consisting of 2 bay leaves and 1 teaspoon
  dried thyme tied together in cheesecloth)
1 tablespoon all-purpose flour mashed together
  with 1 tablespoon butter
2 pounds small white onions, about golf-ball size, peeled
2 tablespoons sugar
1 pound mushroom caps
juice of ½ lemon

1. Preheat the oven to 350°F.

2. Toss the meat with the flour to coat. Discard the flour. Heat 2 tablespoons of the oil and 2 tablespoons of the butter in a large skillet over high heat.

continued

Next spread: **BEEF BOURGUIGNONNE WITH MUSHROOMS AND PEARL ONIONS ON KEVEN'S PILAF WITH MIXED GREENS WITH CHERRY TOMATOES**

This stew can be made a day or two ahead.

The mushrooms and onions should be added at the very end so that they retain their color. They don't have to go into the stew at all; they can be added around the pilaf.

The onions must poach very slowly and gently or the center of the onion will pop.

Add the beef to the skillet in batches and season with the pepper. Add more butter and oil as needed. Sear the meat until brown, about 3 minutes per side. Transfer to a large ovenproof baking dish with a tight-fitting lid.

3. Add the warmed cognac to the skillet and carefully light with a long match, averting your face and keeping long hair and dangling sleeves away from the skillet; cook until the cognac burns out. Deglaze the pan after it is done flaming, using a wooden spoon to scrape up any browned bits on the bottom. Add the cognac mixture to the baking dish with the meat.

4. In the same skillet, fry the bacon over medium-high heat, about 5 minutes. Transfer to a paper towel. Pour off all but 2 tablespoons of fat.

5. Place the garlic, carrots, leeks, onions, and parsley in the bowl of a food processor. Process until finely chopped and add to the bacon fat. Cook over medium-low heat until the vegetables are softened, about 10 minutes. Add the vegetables to the baking dish. Add the bacon as well. Add ½ cup of the wine to the skillet and deglaze the pan further; add the liquid to the baking dish, along with the bouquet garni, and cover. Cook in the oven until the meat is slightly tender, about 1 hour. Stir the flour-butter paste into the baking dish until dissolved and cook until the meat is very tender, another 60 minutes or more if necessary.

6. Heat 2 tablespoons of the butter in a separate skillet over medium heat. Add the small white onions and sprinkle with the sugar; keep cooking until brown, about 5 minutes. Reduce the heat to low and add the remaining ¼ cup wine. Cover and cook until the onions become tender when pierced with a sharp knife, 12 to 15 minutes. Cover the onions to keep them warm.

7. Heat 1 tablespoon of oil in another medium-size skillet over medium-high heat. Cook the mushroom caps until browned, about 4 minutes. Sprinkle the mushrooms with the lemon juice and keep warm. Just before serving, add the onions and mushrooms to the Bourguignonne. Serve with Keven's Pilaf (page 89) or Buttered Noodles (page 99).

KEVEN'S PILAF

Pilaf combines rice with vermicelli pasta, and while you could serve plain rice with Beef Bourguignonne (page 85), I prefer pilaf because it's more interesting and very special. I first tasted this pilaf as a young married woman when I was living in San Francisco in 1960. Keven and I were best of friends and new mothers together. Her mother-in-law was Armenian and she got this recipe from her. Pilaf is especially good with stews, but it also makes a lovely side dish with roasts or grills. Don't think of it as a winter dish; rely on it year-round.

> 4 1/2 cups water
> 1/4 cup strong chicken bouillon or broth
>   (I use Spice Islands)
> 1/4 cup (1/2 stick) butter
> 2 whole coils vermicelli (1/4 pound) or 1/2 cup
>   broken-up thin spaghetti
> 2 cups long-grain rice

1. Preheat the oven to 425°F.

2. In a medium-size saucepan, bring the water to a boil with the bouillon. Remove from the heat. Meanwhile, melt the butter in a large ovenproof saucepan over medium-high heat and cook the vermicelli until golden brown, about 4 minutes. Add the rice and stir until it becomes opaque and milky white, about 4 minutes. Pour the chicken broth into the saucepan and stir well.

3. Cover and bake in the oven for 20 minutes. Keep warm until serving.

ELLEN'S TIPS

The secret to this is 425°F for 20 minutes—it's like clockwork.

The other secret is that if you need to hold the pilaf for an hour or more, bake for 10 minutes, turn off the heat, and leave the casserole in the oven to hold for up to 45 minutes. It will not dry out this way and it will be hot enough to serve.

Vermicelli sometimes comes in a coil about the size of small apple. There are 4 to 6 of these in a package.

MIXED GREENS
WITH CHERRY TOMATOES

ELLEN'S TIP

Be sure to tear the lettuce leaves into manageable bite-size pieces.

A big salad, whether it is this one or another one of your own making, is key to this menu. You want something crisp, clean-tasting, and simple. Avoid adding anything to it—you don't want too much going on. I prefer to use a mixture of assorted lettuce greens and add tomatoes for color. As for a dressing, use Ellen's Dressing (page 232) or a vinaigrette of your own.

> *2 heads Boston lettuce*
> *2 Belgian endive, washed, cored, and split lengthwise*
> *1 medium-size cucumber, peeled and sliced*
> *1 teaspoon dried basil*
> *1/2 teaspoon dried oregano*
> *14 to 16 cherry tomatoes, served whole or cut in half, depending on size*
> *1/2 cup Ellen's salad dressing or one of your choice*

1. Choose the very best and sweetest leaves from the lettuce. Trim the lettuce, then wash and drain or spin-dry. Wrap the leaves loosely in paper towels until you are ready to use them, or put them directly in your salad bowl and cover with a clean, dry dish towel. Add the endive, cucumber slices, dried herbs, and tomatoes and refrigerate.

2. Toss the salad with the dressing before you are ready to serve.

ANGEL FOOD CAKE WITH
SLICED PEARS,
CRÈME ANGLAISE,
AND FRESH NUTMEG

I don't much like plain angel food cake, but when you top it with sliced fresh pears and a silky custard sauce, it's divine. Be sure to have ripe pears and fresh nutmeg and a grater on the table. A dusting of freshly grated nutmeg will bring out the flavor of the pears. Don't be intimidated by the cake because you think that angel food cakes can be made only by professional bakers. Not true. Anyone can make this cake successfully.

MAKES ONE 9-INCH CAKE

1 cup all-purpose flour, sifted
1½ cups confectioners' sugar, sifted
12 large egg whites, at room temperature
1½ teaspoons cream of tartar
¼ teaspoon salt
1 cup granulated sugar
1½ teaspoons pure vanilla extract
6 ripe pears (Bartletts are best), cored, peeled,
    and thinly sliced
Crème Anglaise (page 93)
1 nutmeg

1. Preheat the oven to 375°F.

2. Combine the flour and confectioners' sugar in a medium-size bowl and set aside. Using an electric mixer on high speed, beat the egg whites, cream of tartar, and salt together in a large bowl until frothy. Add the granulated sugar little by little, beating constantly until soft, shiny peaks form. Add the vanilla and beat again to mix well. When you lift the beaters, the peaks should remain stiff. Gently fold in the flour-and-sugar mixture using a large spatula until completely combined (see Ellen's Tips).

3. Pour the batter into an ungreased tube pan and cut through the batter with a knife to remove any air pockets.

continued

Let your eggs come to room temperature before you make this cake or when you do any baking. Room-temperature eggs achieve greater volume when beaten and cook more evenly.

If your angel food cake doesn't rise, it might be because the batter wasn't folded properly. To "fold," you need a clean spatula and you need to follow these directions: First, add the flour by the tablespoon to the stiff egg whites and begin to fold, using a "U"-shaped cutting motion. Cut down to the bottom of the bowl with the long edge of the spatula, then scrape the bottom and come back up, forming a "U" shape. Always use the long side of the spatula to fold as much batter as possible. Keep turning the bowl as you fold in the dry ingredients. Folding keeps air in the egg whites, which is necessary for height.

The cake can be made 1 day in advance and kept wrapped tightly in plastic wrap after it has cooled completely.

4. Bake until the cake has risen to the top of the pan and is golden brown, 30 to 35 minutes. Invert on a funnel or over a bottle to cool.

5. When cool to the touch, use a serrated knife to remove the cake from the tube pan. Carefully cut around the center of the funnel part to loosen the cake completely from the pan. Invert the cake onto a cake plate.

6. To serve, cut the cake into 8 to 10 slices. Top each slice of cake with 5 to 6 slices of pears and a ladle of Crème Anglaise. Grate some fresh nutmeg on top to garnish.

CRÈME ANGLAISE

MAKES 2 CUPS

1 1/2 cups half-and-half
1/2 vanilla bean, split lengthwise
6 large egg yolks, at room temperature
2/3 cup sugar

1. Place the half-and-half and vanilla bean in a medium-size saucepan over medium heat. Bring to a boil and remove from the heat. Take out the vanilla bean, and scrape out the inside seeds of the pod using the rounded edge of a knife. Put the vanilla seeds back into the half-and-half mixture and discard the pod.

2. Using an electric mixer set on high speed or a whisk, beat the egg yolks in a medium-size bowl until pale yellow. Gradually add the sugar and beat for 3 minutes longer, until they are light and thick. Add 2 tablespoons of the hot half-and-half to the egg yolks and mix lightly. Add another 2 tablespoons and mix until the egg yolks and half-and-half are completely combined. Add the egg yolk mixture to the saucepan with the remaining half-and-half and cook over medium heat, whisking constantly until the mixture begins to thicken, about 5 minutes. It should coat a metal spoon when lifted out. Strain through a fine sieve. Let cool, then refrigerate overnight, covered.

ANGEL FOOD CAKE WITH SLICED PEARS,
CRÈME ANGLAISE, AND FRESH NUTMEG

If you have a real angel food cake knife, which looks like long spokes on a bar, that is great. I have never owned one and I use a serrated knife, which works just fine. Use the knife to lightly saw the cake. Don't press.

Squeeze some fresh lemon juice on the sliced pears to keep them from turning brown.

If the custard becomes lumpy and looks like scrambled eggs, whisk in 1 tablespoon boiling water to smooth it out.

Remember, the brown specks that come from the vanilla bean are a wonderful indication that you made the Crème Anglaise with a real vanilla bean. You can use 1 1/2 teaspoons of vanilla extract instead, but it isn't nearly as good.

Crème Anglaise can be made a day in advance and kept cold. It should be served at room temperature.

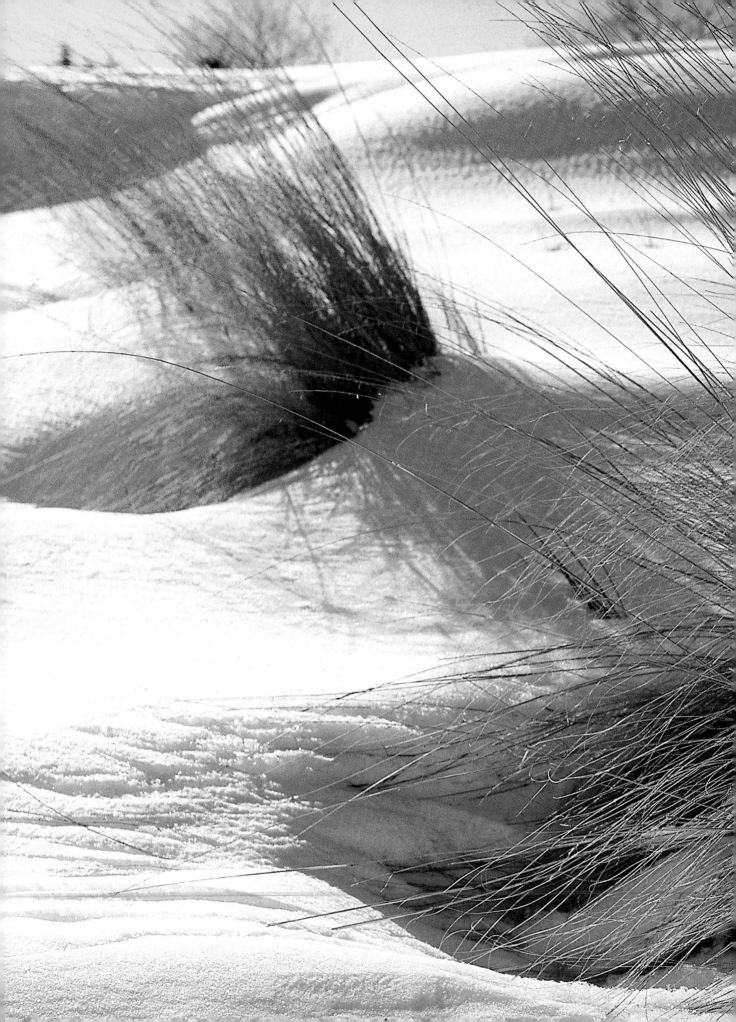

The Czech Family Reunion

SESAME PITA TOASTS

CHICKEN PAPRIKASH

BUTTERED NOODLES

SWEET-AND-SOUR RED CABBAGE

SUSAN'S BOURBON CAKE

Serves 4 to 6

When Joe and I lived in Washington, D.C., his mother came to visit us from Oklahoma. Unbeknownst to us, she had invited all of her long-lost Czech relatives from Maryland and Virginia to dinner. (We were expecting, at most, two couples.) Suddenly, about twenty people descended. There was lots of hugging and laughing and reminiscing, all of it in this Slavic language. I felt totally out of place since I didn't understand one word. All I could do was try to be charming and helpful. I remember wandering around, filling up glasses and removing plates and smiling a lot,

looking lost. They, on the other hand, were quite happy, especially Ann Wright.

Joe's mom called him Bobby as a young boy to distinguish him from his dad, also Joe, and all the Czech relatives called him Bobby, too. To this day, Christmas cards arrive addressed to Bobby and Ellen Wright, wishing us well in Czech!

Eventually, the evening ended and they all went home, and it was then that I realized what an insane but fun time we had had. This recipe for Chicken Paprikash (opposite) is straight from the old country and is very tasty. So is Mama Wright's Sweet-

and-Sour Red Cabbage (page 100).

Mama Wright died before we'd finished our home in Bridgehampton and I miss her all the time. She would have loved the wide-open feeling about it—the stone fireplaces and the fields. And she would have particularly loved the kitchen, which works like a dream. She had an intriguing theory on why certain kitchens didn't work, and she wasn't shy about telling you: "Must have been designed by a man," she'd state, and, you know, almost without exception, she was right.

We like to have a cold, dry Pinot Grigio with this meal.

CHICKEN PAPRIKASH

This is a dish straight from Mama Wright. Over many a bridge game we discussed food and cooking. She shared a lot of her recipes with me and I took them gladly because she was a very good cook. She gave me recipes from Czechoslovakia, along with some great stories about the war and how difficult it was to get things like sour cream and eggs. She couldn't have made this paprikash back then. You can prepare this dish the day before you plan to serve it, all the way up to the point of adding the sour cream. Add the sour cream just before you serve it and be careful not to let it overheat or the sour cream will break up (see Ellen's Tips).

one 5- to 6-pound chicken, cut into serving pieces
1/2 cup paprika
3 tablespoons canola oil
3 medium-size onions, chopped
2 ribs celery, trimmed and chopped
2 medium-size carrots, chopped
1/2 green bell pepper, seeded and finely chopped (optional)
2 cups chicken broth (canned is fine)
one 16-ounce container sour cream
Buttered Noodles (page 99)
Sweet-and-Sour Red Cabbage (page 100)

There are many different kinds of paprika, some sweet, some spicy, and some aromatic. If you are lucky enough to live near a Hungarian store, you can try them all and see which one you like best. I prefer sweet for this dish.

Paprika, like all spices, loses its flavor over time, so make sure your paprika is freshly purchased. Paprika is best when used within 6 months of purchase.

1. Preheat the oven to 350°F.

2. Wash and dry the chicken pieces and sprinkle heavily with the paprika. Heat 2 tablespoons of the oil in a large skillet over medium-high heat. Cook the pieces, a few at a time, until brown, about 5 minutes per side, and transfer to a 3-quart casserole. Continue to cook the chicken in this manner, using the last tablespoon of oil when you need it.

3. Reduce the heat under the skillet to medium and add the onions, celery, carrots, and green pepper. Cook, stirring, until soft, about 5 minutes, and add to the casserole with the chicken. Add the chicken broth to barely cover. Reserve any extra.

4. Bake until the chicken is tender, adding more broth if necessary, about 45 minutes. Gently pour some of the liquid into a medium-size bowl. Whisk the sour cream into the cooking liquid until smooth. Pour the mixture back into the casserole and stir to combine.

5. Serve over Buttered Noodles to sop up the sauce. Sweet-and-Sour Red Cabbage completes the meal.

BUTTERED NOODLES

Given that you will have made the Chicken Paprikash (page 97) (which is the reason for serving these noodles) ahead of time, I'd delay cooking these until just before you plan to serve them. That way, they will be perfect. And be sure to use a big enough pot with ample water. One pound of noodles is almost enough for four.

> 2 quarts water
> ½ teaspoon salt
> 1 teaspoon vegetable or olive oil
> two 1-pound bags wide egg noodles
> ¼ cup (½ stick) butter
> 3 tablespoons chopped fresh parsley leaves
> (optional)

1. Bring the water to a boil in a large pot over high heat. Add the salt, oil, and noodles. Reduce the heat to medium and stir the noodles to mix them thoroughly with the oil. Cook until the noodles are soft but not mushy, and slightly chewy, about 5 minutes. Take out a noodle and bite it to check the consistency.

2. Drain the noodles in a colander and put them in a large, warm bowl. Add the butter and toss. Keep warm. Garnish with the chopped parsley if desired.

**CHICKEN PAPRIKASH
ON BUTTERED NOODLES**

ELLEN'S TIPS

Don't let the noodles sit longer than 30 minutes before eating. Even if you keep them warm, they tend to stick together soon after cooking.

Chopped chives or sliced scallions are also a good garnish instead of parsley.

Noodles that are soft but still slightly resistant when chewed are referred to by Italians as al dente, which translates literally into "to the tooth."

SWEET-AND-SOUR RED CABBAGE

ELLEN'S TIP

I suggest seasoning to taste with the sugar and vinegar; some people like the cabbage more tart than others.

Joe's mother gave me this recipe to accompany meat and chicken dishes. I like it best alongside Chicken Paprikash (page 97), but it's also very good with other meat dishes. You must prepare it at the last minute, just before serving, for it to be perfect.

2 tablespoons butter
1 head red cabbage, cored and thinly sliced
¼ cup chicken broth (canned is fine)
3 tablespoons sugar
3 tablespoons good-quality red wine vinegar

Heat the butter in a large skillet over medium-high heat. Add the cabbage and cook, stirring, until it is wilted, about 6 minutes, then add the remaining ingredients. Cover and cook until tender, about 5 minutes.

SUSAN'S BOURBON CAKE

I love to make desserts of all kinds—pies and cakes, cobblers and puddings. They end a meal with a bang. This one is a great cake—a beautiful Bundt cake from my dear friend Susan Brinkley, who is a very good cook. It is perfectly flavored with bourbon, in both the batter and the glaze. The cake is so dense and caramel in color, it feels and looks like you're eating suede.

MAKES ONE 10-INCH BUNDT CAKE

For the cake

1½ cups (3 sticks) butter, at room temperature,
    plus more for the pan and the wax paper
½ cup plain dried bread crumbs
3¼ cups firmly packed light brown sugar
3½ cups sifted all-purpose flour
1½ teaspoons baking powder
5 large eggs
¾ cup milk
1 tablespoon pure vanilla extract
½ teaspoon ground mace
¼ cup bourbon

For the glaze

⅓ cup granulated sugar
¼ cup bourbon

1. Preheat the oven to 350°F.

1. Preheat the oven to 350°F.

2. Butter the inside of a 10-inch Bundt pan and set aside. Butter one side of a 16-inch round of wax paper and fit it into the Bundt pan, butter side up, making a hole in the middle to fit the sides and bottom. Use another small piece of wax paper around the funnel (the wax paper won't fit exactly). Sprinkle the bread crumbs into the pan, knocking the excess out. Set the pan aside.

3. Using an electric mixer at medium speed, beat the butter and sugar together in a large bowl until smooth. In a small bowl, combine the flour and baking powder. In another small bowl, mix the eggs and milk together. Alternately add to the butter and sugar the flour mixture and the egg mixture and combine until smooth, about 10 minutes (see Ellen's Tips). Add the vanilla, mace, and bourbon and continue to mix another 4 to 5 minutes, until combined.

continued

ELLEN'S TIPS

Beat the batter for this cake at least 10 minutes. This yields the best results. The longer, the better.

Be sure to heat the glaze over the lowest heat possible. It overcooks very quickly and can become really hard to apply.

4. Pour the batter into the prepared Bundt pan and bake until golden brown, until a tester inserted in the center of the cake comes out clean, 70 to 80 minutes. Remove the cake and allow to cool slightly, about 20 minutes. Unmold the cake on a serving plate and peel off the wax paper. Prepare to glaze it while it is still warm.

5. To make the glaze, place the sugar and bourbon in a small saucepan over low heat (see Ellen's Tips) and cook until the sugar is dissolved, about 3 minutes. Paint the glaze on the warm cake with a pastry brush or drizzle it on with a spoon.

New Year's Eve Dinner

MEREDITH'S CAVIAR PIE

LEG OF LAMB WITH FRESH MINT SAUCE

AND ROASTED POTATOES

GLAZED CARROTS

ANNE DONAHOE'S CHOCOLATE ROLL

Serves 8

New Year's Eve has never been my favorite thing. The idea of watching the countdown of the ball dropping in Times Square is even worse. I love that my kids like to go to parties and carry on, but I have never been one to do so, even when I was younger. I don't know why, but this fact has propelled me to create a different type of celebration, one that is quiet and classy and ends when anyone wants it to.

Thank God Joe agrees with me. We like to be with a few good friends or family and have a lovely dinner, drink some great champagne—like good chilled Dom Pérignon—in pretty champagne glasses, and go to bed before midnight. Bridgehampton truly lends itself to just that.

With an evening that is low key, the food must be great, and this menu is. It begins with Meredith's Caviar Pie (page 104), a sour cream and caviar combination given to me by Meredith Brokaw that I could personally devour all by myself. It is rich and elegant and goes beautifully with champagne—all in all, just the right note on which to

start. Leg of lamb is the main attraction, with all the expected bells and whistles—crunchy roasted potatoes, buttery glazed carrots, and fresh mint sauce. Serve this with a Rhône wine; a 1985 or 1993 vintage would be very special. Chocolate roll served with a hot fudge sauce completes the meal. A sip of champagne with the chocolate roll wouldn't be a bad touch either.

Have a very happy new year, however you may want to celebrate it. If you're like us, your tummy will be humming and your eyes will be shut before the witching hour.

MEREDITH'S CAVIAR PIE

ELLEN'S TIPS

*Osetra and Sevruga caviar
are very good caviars.
Beluga is of course the
best caviar, but not
really necessary here.*

*Use your fingers or knuckles
to press the chopped
egg into the pie plate.*

*Slice the scallions into
small, neat rounds using
mostly the green. It looks
prettier that way.*

*Another way to serve this
delicious pie is to take
small russet potatoes, rub
them with olive oil, and
bake in a 375°F oven.
When they are tender,
halve them and scoop out
the center. Put the shells
back in the oven and bake
until they are crisp, then
use the shells as a container
for a dollop of caviar, a
spoonful of chopped egg,
and a spoonful of sour
cream mixture.*

You don't need the most expensive caviar for this hors d'oeuvre or first course. It is made of chopped eggs, sour cream, scallions, and caviar, all artfully assembled. A good caviar will do. If you're having caviar plain or with just a touch of chopped egg, that's when you need the best you can find. I like to serve this with Melba rounds or small toast points.

MAKES ONE 9-INCH PIE

8 hard-boiled eggs, peeled, cooled, and cut into pieces
½ cup (1 stick) butter, melted
1 pint sour cream
4 scallions, trimmed and chopped (see Ellen's Tips)
4 ounces caviar—Sevruga, Osetra, or Beluga

1. In a large bowl, mash the eggs finely with a fork and mix in the melted butter. Spread evenly in a 9-inch pie plate, covering the bottom and the sides about ¼ inch thick with the mixture. Spread the sour cream in the bottom and chill for at least 2 hours.

2. Decorate with the chopped scallions around the edge of the pie plate to create a 1-inch green border. Just before serving, mound the caviar in the center. The end result is a white sour cream background, green chopped scallion border, and a black round of caviar in the middle.

3. Cut into wedges for a first course and serve with Melba rounds, small toast triangles, or even potato skins (see Ellen's Tips).

MEREDITH'S CAVIAR PIE

Leg of Lamb with Fresh Mint Sauce and Roasted Potatoes

ELLEN'S TIPS

After the lamb is removed from the oven, it will cook a bit more, so don't over-cook it. Nothing is worse than a gray leg of lamb.

I suggest you make the mint sauce a day or more in advance so it can chill completely. It will reduce your workload on the day of your party as well.

At one point in my cooking career, for something as special as a New Year's Eve dinner, I would have set aside 3 days for cooking. Day one would have entailed making brioche dough and duxelles. Day two, I'd roll and stuff the leg of lamb with the duxelles. Day three, I'd wrap the leg in the brioche, then decorate the brioche with hand-cut brioche leaves. That is how I learned to cook—nothing was too hard—but that is not how I cook anymore. People I know want easy but good recipes. A tried-and-true, simple, well-prepared roast is what I like to make now. You season the meat carefully, put it into the oven, leave the kitchen, and when you come back the entrée is done. Keep it simple, don't overcook it, and be sure to make the fresh mint sauce. It bears no resemblance at all to mint jelly. If you've never had fresh mint sauce, you've got to try it.

Let the roast sit for 5 minutes before carving. Hold the bone with one hand and carve away from it to slice. You get more meat that way.

For the mint sauce

1 cup white vinegar
1/3 cup sugar
1 cup fresh mint leaves, chopped

For the leg of lamb

one 5-pound leg of lamb, trimmed of excess fat
2 tablespoons coarse salt
4 cloves garlic, thinly sliced
2 medium-size onions, sliced
24 new red potatoes, scrubbed

1. Put the vinegar and sugar in a small saucepan over medium-high heat and boil for 10 minutes. Add the chopped mint, reduce the heat to low, and simmer for 5 minutes. Chill completely.

2. Preheat the oven to 425°F.

3. Rub the leg of lamb with 1 tablespoon of the salt and make five to seven 1-inch-deep slits in the meat. Insert the slices of garlic into the slits. Place the onion slices in the bottom of a large roasting pan and add the lamb. Roast,

uncovered, for 20 minutes. Reduce the oven temperature to 350°F and continue to cook an additional 40 minutes.

4. Place the new potatoes around the meat and sprinkle with the remaining 1 tablespoon salt. Baste them with some pan drippings. Cook until a meat thermometer inserted in the center of the lamb reads 145° to 148°F for medium rare, another 40 to 45 minutes. Let sit for 5 minutes, then carve and serve with the chilled mint sauce.

GLAZED CARROTS
WITH ALMONDS

These carrots look as if they have been roasted alongside the lamb, as some recipes suggest, but, in fact, they are cooked in an entirely different manner. First, you parboil them, then cook them in a mixture of butter and sugar, which makes carrots sweeter. They should really be cooked soft. This is one recipe where a little overcooking is allowed. Add the almonds right at the end; you want the contrast of the crunchy nuts and tender carrots.

8 medium-size carrots, thinly sliced
pinch of salt
¼ cup (½ stick) butter
1 tablespoon sugar
3 tablespoons slivered blanched almonds, toasted
(optional; see Ellen's Tips)

1. Place the carrots and salt in a medium-size saucepan and cover with water. Bring to a boil over high heat and cook until tender, about 15 minutes. Drain the carrots and set aside.

2. Heat the butter in a medium-size skillet over medium heat and cook the carrots until they are coated with butter. Sprinkle the sugar over the carrots and shake the skillet so they are uniformly coated. Cover the skillet and cook until the carrots brown, about 4 minutes, shaking the skillet from time to time. The carrots should be a lovely shade of deep orange.

3. If you are adding the almonds, stir them in now and serve.

ELLEN'S TIPS

The carrots may need more time to brown in the sugar-and-butter mixture. The best way to judge is to check them occasionally and remove them only when they are deep orange.

To toast the nuts, place them on a cookie sheet or toaster oven tray and bake at 300°F for 2 to 3 minutes, until golden brown.

ANNE DONAHOE'S CHOCOLATE ROLL

Bring eggs to room temperature when you bake. Your cakes will be bigger and better.

James Beard taught his students to "fold" with their hands! Be sure that the chocolate cake batter has no white streaks in it and is fully folded. Although I use a spatula to fold, I have done it with my hands to get the feel of it. It's a good thing to try sometime.

Feel free enough to mold the roll with your hands, as I explained in the recipe. Your fingers can and should be used without being afraid!

You can make this in the morning, refrigerate it all day, and serve that night.

When my son, David, was three, I went to pick him up from a play date with a pal of his by the name of Daniel Donahoe. I didn't know the Donahoes well at all and was touched when Anne invited me in for coffee and cake. I was expecting a piece of pound or loaf cake. Instead, Anne Donahoe gave me the cake she had served the night before. It was (and is) unlike any other chocolate roll I have ever tasted. It's made with seven ounces of melted Eagle brand chocolate, has a whipped cream filling, and Hot Fudge Sauce as a topping. If you're going to celebrate—it is New Year's Eve, after all—this is the way to top off your perfect meal.

> *2 tablespoons unsalted butter at room temperature*
> *7 ounces sweet milk chocolate (I use Eagle brand)*
> *6 tablespoons strong brewed coffee, cooled*
> *7 large eggs, separated*
> *1¼ cups sugar*
> *3 tablespoons unsweetened cocoa powder (I use Hershey's)*
> *1 cup heavy cream, whipped to soft peaks*

1. Preheat the oven to 375°F.

2. Butter an 11 × 17-inch jelly roll pan with the 2 tablespoons of softened butter, line it with wax paper, and butter the wax paper. Set aside.

3. Put the chocolate and coffee in a microwave-safe bowl and melt, about 1 minute. Let cool for at least 10 minutes. Using an electric mixer on medium-high, beat the egg yolks with ¾ cup of the sugar in a large bowl until pale yellow, about 3 minutes. Then beat the chocolate with coffee into the egg yolk mixture. In another large bowl, beat the egg whites with an electric mixer on high speed until stiff peaks form, about 4 minutes. Gently fold the whites into the chocolate mixture using a large spatula until no white streaks remain (see Ellen's Tips). Pour the batter evenly into the jelly roll pan.

4. Bake in the center of the oven for 10 minutes. Turn off the oven and let the cake sit for 5 minutes with the door shut.

5. Remove the cake and place in the refrigerator until the bottom of the pan is cool to the touch, about 10 minutes.

continued

ANNE DONAHOE'S CHOCOLATE ROLL

6. While the cake is chilling, place a clean, dry dish towel on a flat surface and sprinkle the towel with the remaining $\frac{1}{2}$ cup sugar.

7. Take the chocolate cake out of the refrigerator. Sift the cocoa generously on top of the cake. Invert the cake onto the sugared towel to unmold. Carefully and slowly pull off the wax paper. Spread the cake evenly about $\frac{1}{2}$ inch high with the whipped cream, leaving 2 inches to spare around the edges. Then start to roll the cake up lengthwise with the help of the dish towel. Don't be afraid to use your hands to shape the roll. The cake may crack sometimes but it will still roll. Put the roll seam side down on a surface that suits the shape of the roll, such as a long plate, board, or tray. Shape it with your hands, making it round and even. Chill until serving, at least 1 hour. Serve it with Hot Fudge Sauce (recipe follows), either ladling a spoonful of it over each slice or passing it separately in a sauceboat.

HOT FUDGE SAUCE

6 ounces unsweetened chocolate
1 cup half-and-half
1$\frac{1}{2}$ cups sugar
1 teaspoon pure vanilla extract

1. Put the chocolate, half-and-half, sugar, and vanilla into a medium-size microwave-safe bowl, and microwave on medium-high to melt, about 3 minutes. When the chocolate is fully melted, beat with a spoon until smooth. The sauce can be reheated in the microwave on medium heat for 30 seconds just before serving.

2. Serve in a pretty sauceboat with your fanciest ladle.

Valentine's Day Dinner

PUFF PASTRY STICKS

LAMB SHANKS WITH WHITE BEANS

HOT CRUSTY BREAD

MUSTARD GREENS

RED VELVET CAKE

Serves 6 to 8

I don't know exactly why I think of Valentine's Day as a dressy occasion but I do, with lovely red cranberry balls for the table and silver gourds and cut crystal. That's not to say that I'm not doing what everybody else has been doing, too—sending off Valentines to my children and grandchildren.

We celebrate Valentine's Day with a delicious dinner for a few good friends. Hopefully there is a blanket of snow on the ground to provide a pretty background. By necessity, it is a wintry menu that will end on a very special note, with a red (and it is really red) cake for dessert. Sometimes I decorate the table with small vases of red roses, cut short. Tall anything on the table, with the exception of candles, is one of my pet peeves. You can't see the people and you can't talk through them. If the goal is a gorgeous arrangement, a prominent place for it can be found somewhere else. Floating flowers are my favorite, or several pots of violets.

The Valentine's Day menu that follows adheres to my general rules for success: Start with something yummy—Puff Pastry Sticks (page 115). Concentrate most of your effort and time on one dish—the lamb shanks. Keep the accompaniments simple and they

will take care of themselves. Finish with something divine that your friends will go home remembering—Red Velvet Cake (page 119).

Valentine's Day is all about love and food that is carefully prepared is the best Valentine you can give.

Serve with a good Italian Barolo or a Brunello.

PUFF PASTRY STICKS

Although I have made classic puff pastry and liked the challenge of it, frozen puff pastry, available in supermarkets, works like a dream. These sticks are light and crispy and have just the right taste and texture for the big meal to follow. Make them ahead if you want to, but be sure to keep them in an airtight container. Cut the pastry sheets into four 6-inch-long sticks about ½ inch wide. Sprinkle them with either freshly grated Parmesan cheese or paprika (or both) and bake for 7 to 8 minutes in a preheated 400°F oven until golden brown.

LAMB SHANKS WITH WHITE BEANS

This is a wonderful recipe that I received on E-mail from a friend and that I like to serve when it's cold outside. As with many braises and stews, you can count on it tasting better with time, so you should make it in the morning and let it sit with the cover ajar for a while to absorb the flavors, or prepare it 1 day in advance and refrigerate. The combination of tender white beans and even more tender lamb is very special. Serve it with hot French bread and a nice green vegetable, and you've got a fabulous meal.

> *5 large cloves garlic, crushed*
> *1 large onion, diced*
> *4 medium-size carrots, diced*
> *3 ribs celery, trimmed and diced*
> *6 lamb shanks (about 1 pound each)*
> *salt and freshly ground black pepper to taste*
> *3 tablespoons olive oil*
> *1 cup good quality red wine*
> *8 cups chicken broth (canned is fine)*
> *one 28-ounce can whole plum tomatoes, drained*
> *one 14-ounce can crushed tomatoes, with their liquid*
> *3 sprigs fresh rosemary*
> *2 bay leaves*
> *1 pound dried Great Northern beans, white beans,*
> *   or lima beans, rinsed, picked over, soaked overnight*
> *   in cold water, and drained*

1. Place the garlic, onion, carrots, and celery in the bowl of a food processor and dice. Transfer to a small bowl and set aside.

2. Generously season the lamb with salt and pepper. Heat the olive oil in a deep, large skillet over medium-high heat. Add the lamb and cook until browned, about 3 minutes per side. Transfer the lamb to a plate and pour off all but 1 tablespoon of the oil.

3. Add the minced vegetables to the skillet and cook over medium heat, stirring, until soft, about 5 minutes. Pour in the wine and cook until all the vegetables are tender, about 8 minutes. Return the lamb shanks to the skillet and add the chicken broth. Increase the heat to high and add the tomatoes, rosemary, bay leaves, and beans. Bring to a boil, reduce the heat to low, and simmer, covered, for about 2 hours, until the meat is quite tender and falls off the bone. Remove the bay leaves and rosemary sprigs and discard them.

HOT CRUSTY BREAD

ELLEN'S TIPS

This method of heating bread makes it crisp on the outside and moist and soft on the inside.

Be careful not to soak the loaf of bread in water.

Be careful not to leave the bread in the oven too long or it will dry out.

Italian or sourdough bread can be substituted for the baguette.

After the bread is warmed, don't cover it with a towel or it will get soggy.

I like to pack the butter for the bread in a small ramekin while it is soft so that when I serve it, it looks neat and shiny. It must be refrigerated, however, so it's cool when served. Garnish the ramekin with a small leaf of parsley or coriander on the top.

For a butter variation, try 2 tablespoons strawberry jam mixed with ½ cup (1 stick) softened butter.

This isn't a recipe, it's a trick, in a way—to make an extra-crispy loaf of French bread. To serve it, cut it into slices on the diagonal and put them in a basket lined with a cloth napkin. On the side, I serve a ramekin of butter that I like to flavor. To one stick softened butter, add either 2 tablespoons minced fresh parsley leaves or 1 tablespoon each chopped garlic and fresh rosemary needles.

1 French baguette
½ cup (1 stick) butter

1. Preheat the oven to 400°F.
2. Take the loaf of bread and run it very quickly under cold running water so that the crust of the bread is slightly damp. Bake it in the center of the oven until crispy, 8 to 10 minutes. Cut ½-inch-thick slices diagonally and put the slices into a bread basket lined with a large napkin or cloth towel. Serve with butter.

MUSTARD GREENS

I happen to love eating different kinds of greens—mustard greens, collard greens, turnip greens, spinach—and the more I read about them, the more inclined I am to cook them. They are full of vitamins and recommended all the time for strong bones and good health. Whichever greens you prefer, this recipe for mustard greens works well for all the dark, leafy greens.

2 bunches mustard greens (about 2 pounds)
2 tablespoons extra-virgin olive oil
salt and freshly ground pepper to taste

1. Wash the greens thoroughly in cold water; they tend to be sandy. Shake off any excess water but do not dry the greens entirely. Trim the stems.
2. Heat a large skillet over high heat and add the greens a little at a time. Stir them as they wilt, adding more greens. Drizzle the olive oil over the greens and cover the skillet for a few seconds. This whole cooking period takes no more than 4 minutes. As soon as the greens are wilted, remove them from the skillet, season with salt and pepper, and serve immediately.

RED VELVET CAKE

Here is a wonderful cake—the perfect one for Valentine's Day—from Theresa, my daughter Claudia's southern friend, who has good taste when it comes to baked things. This two-layer beauty is also made with buttermilk, which keeps it moist. This cake is knockout red, and it is crowned with white, fluffy Cream Cheese Frosting. Some people garnish the top with pecan halves.

ELLEN'S TIP

The cooking of mustard greens is so quick that you can have everything ready to cook and begin cooking the greens just before sitting down to eat. They will hold in a warm oven, lightly covered with foil, up to 20 minutes, but if you are planning to do that, undercook them a bit.

MAKES ONE 2-LAYER 9-INCH CAKE

1 teaspoon white vinegar
1 teaspoon baking soda
1 cup buttermilk
2½ cups self-rising flour, plus extra for the cake pan
1 tablespoon unsweetened cocoa powder
½ teaspoon salt
1½ cups vegetable oil, plus extra for the cake pan
1½ cups sugar
2 large eggs
2 tablespoons red food coloring
1 teaspoon pure vanilla extract
Cream Cheese Frosting (page 121)
1 cup pecan halves (optional)

1. Preheat the oven to 300°F.

2. In a medium-size mixing bowl, combine the vinegar, baking soda, and buttermilk. In a second medium-size mixing bowl, sift together the flour, cocoa, and salt.

3. Grease and flour two 9-inch cake pans. Tap out any excess flour. In a large mixing bowl, combine the oil, sugar, and eggs. Beat with an electric mixer on high speed for 3 to 4 minutes, until thickened.

4. Alternately add to the egg mixture the flour mixture and the buttermilk mixture, beating for at least 2 to 3 minutes after each addition. When all the ingredients have been added to the bowl, beat another 3 to 4 minutes on high speed.

5. Mix in the red food coloring and vanilla until smooth. Divide the batter equally between the 2 cake pans and bake on center rack until a tester inserted in the

center of the cake comes out clean, about 45 minutes. Cool 5 to 10 minutes in the pan. Turn out onto a wire rack and let cool completely before frosting.

6. Frost the first round on top about $\frac{1}{2}$ inch thick with frosting, avoiding the edges by about $\frac{1}{2}$ inch. Put the second round on top and press slightly to line it up with the first round. Frost the sides, then the top.

7. Decorate with pecan halves, if desired.

ELLEN'S TIP

If you have an uneven cake, chop some pecans and put a layer all around the sides of the cake. This fixes the "lean" because your eye can't see it anymore.

CREAM CHEESE FROSTING

one 8-ounce package cream cheese, at room temperature
$\frac{1}{2}$ cup (1 stick) unsalted butter, at room temperature
one 16-ounce box confectioners' sugar
1 teaspoon pure vanilla extract

1. Place all of the ingredients in a medium-size mixing bowl and mix with an electric mixer on high speed for 3 to 4 minutes until completely combined and smooth.

2. If made 1 day ahead of time, the frosting can be covered with plastic wrap and refrigerated; it should be brought to room temperature before frosting the cake.

RED VELVET CAKE

SPRING

S P R I N G

When I stop to think about spring, the first signs of it don't happen in Bridgehampton at all. They happen in New York City, on the tiny terrace of our apartment, of all places. My husband is an insane gardener—a farmer at heart—who, well before the frost has thawed on Long Island, starts his own plants from seeds. Some late-winter afternoon I'll come home to our apartment and find battalions of furry little peat pots lined up in the sun. Joe has gotten his tomatoes, radishes, and sunflowers going in anticipation of planting them in the vegetable and flower garden in Bridgehampton sometime around Memorial Day. His prized dahlias, separated and snugly wrapped in burlap, are waiting for him in the basement in Bridgehampton, winterized way back in the fall. The peat pots move into coffee cups as they get bigger and then they need stakes. He obviously likes to make things grow, and I like to see him carefully nurturing these little baby plants. I also love my tub of herbs that he plants each year for me just outside the kitchen door. Something would be missing without all of these plants, and it wouldn't be just about good food.

In Vermont, they call late winter mud season, a wonderful expression. Depending upon the amount of snow and/or rain that has swept across the East End of Long Island during the winter, the ground will likely be muddy and waterlogged, or just plain hard and cold. Even when it thaws, the soil will still be hard, thanks to the good amount of clay in it. As anyone who has tried to work the soil there knows, it takes strong hands and a lot of elbow grease before it will do what you want it to do for you. There is a plus, though. Soil with clay holds moisture and gardeners love that. Things grow amazingly well on the land where we live.

I think of spring as a waiting game: You wait for the last snow to fall, for the earth to thaw, for the days to lengthen, for the interminable rain to stop, for the trees to bud, for the crocuses and daffodils to show their little green beginnings. You wait and you wait and you might have to wait some more, but then one day, all that waiting pays off. There is that tangible change in the air. The wind has shifted. Old Man Winter has gone.

I'm ready for the change. Not that I would ever want to live full time in a climate without winter, but there is a lot to be said for the return of color and flowers and wildlife to the world. If we were to hasten one season along it would be spring. We've been known to invite friends for dinner on the screened-in porch, where we've had cocktails in down vests and sweaters, but try as we might, we end up closing the windows and facing reality—we are rushing Mother Nature and we need to turn the heat on and eat dinner like normal people.

As the temperature changes in spring, so do the kinds of foods I prepare, and I look forward to that, too. From the big stews of winter, I turn to a favorite like Chicken Fricassee with Parsleyed Dumplings (page 133)—also a wonderful one-pot meal. The further it gets into spring, the lighter the food gets, with the sole exceptions of Easter and Memorial Day weekend (the marathon), which demands a meat-and-potatoes meal for runners who have just competed in a 10K race around the potato fields of Bridgehampton and Wainscott. Somehow asparagus quiche just doesn't make it after an effort like that!

I would describe our lives as very casual when it comes to entertaining, but we celebrate Easter Sunday in a kind of formal way, with a more fancy meal, something Joe grew up with and still likes to have. The table will be beautifully set, with crystal and special majolica plates. Instead of lamb, I serve a standing rib roast with Yorkshire pudding—a great favorite in our home, even if it isn't thought of as the usual Easter dinner. There will be some typical spring foods—such as asparagus, eggs, and salmon—in other parts of the meal.

Weekend by weekend, the weather improves. Weekend by weekend, there are more cars on the roads. You cannot help but notice that people are returning to open up

their houses in Bridgehampton after the winter. There is a lot to do in getting the house up and running after the winter.

One of the surest signs of late spring, and one of the most beautiful for us, is when the espaliered apple tree that grows through the deck outside our front door blooms. There may be no more delicate flowers in the world than airy pink apple blossoms. And this lovely tree is home to a bird's nest that looks like a prop stylist put it there. It is one of those perfect round nests that has never had any activity for some reason. It was obviously deserted. Perhaps next year some little bird will use it.

When we renovated our house on Mitchells Lane, we did a lot of things to it,

including moving the driveway from the south side of the house to the east. It meant, among other things, mowing down hundreds of daffodils that had been planted by the previous owner in the field along the old driveway. The next year, the daffodils we had so heartlessly mowed down came back fuller and stronger than ever before—right smack in the middle of our field, a whole sea of daffodils surrounded by clover and green grass.

We landscaped our place deliberately by flower and by color blocks. At the entrance of our driveway on either side, just as you drive in, are orange and yellow daylilies.

You approach the house and the palette changes to white and pink—pink climbing roses on split rail fences, white rhododendrons, pink apple trees, and, just as you get to our front door, four large wine barrels overflowing with pale pink geraniums. They bloom all through the summer, unlike everything else. On the south side of the house is a perennial garden of whites, purples, and pinks. And around the side of the house is Joe's garden, with dahlias that bloom in a variety of pure colors, along with sunflowers of different heights, sizes, and colors. Spring. You can almost taste it—like a good meal.

First Spring Dinner
on the Screened-In Porch

TOMATO PHYLLO PIZZA

CHICKEN FRICASSEE WITH PARSLEYED DUMPLINGS

BUTTER LETTUCE SALAD

RHUBARB AND YOGURT PARFAITS

Serves 6 to 8

Never mind what the calendar says, it's spring to us—the first time we brave the elements and open up the screened-in porch area to have dinner there, with the breeze blowing gently through. We have a long old pine table and while we are eating we can see this heavenly expanse of grass and endless white fences. The view overlooking the fields is lovely with what I've come to think of as "our" horses, even if they are not! There is the most wonderful springtime smell that comes from the thaw, promising blossoms and flowers and the return of longer light-filled days.

This is one of my all-time favorite meals. It's elegant but simple. It's easy to prepare and cooks in a casserole, but you'd never think "easy" from its flavor and different textures. It has an old-fashioned way about it that reminds me of the kind of food my family has always loved. Fricassee—even the word sounds good. I deliberately serve this menu to people in need of comfort food (I guess that includes everyone), and I serve it in big bowls to be eaten with spoons. A knife or fork too, but spoons to get all the good gravy.

Originally rhubarb was available only in spring, when it came up as one of spring's first plants, and was invariably used in pies and cobblers with strawberries, which offset its tart taste. Now rhubarb is sold almost year-round. That doesn't stop me from thinking of it as a spring fruit, but it is really considered a vegetable. I always make rhubarb and yogurt parfaits in spring, because in spring the rhubarb stalks are very pink and pretty.

Serve with a good chilled Chardonnay.

TOMATO PHYLLO PIZZA

Phyllo, if you have never used it before, is easier to work with than you might think. Pizza dough involves yeast and risings and, while it is fun to make, it takes time. Phyllo dough, on the other hand, simply needs to be removed from the box, cut, brushed with butter, arranged, then topped. You can prepare this pizza up to 6 hours ahead; leave it at room temperature, and reheat it for only 10 minutes in a preheated 325°F oven. You'll find that people want to make an entire meal of it. You will need a feather brush or a very soft pastry brush to prepare this recipe.

> *5 tablespoons butter, melted, plus extra for the cookie sheet*
> *one 17-ounce package phyllo pastry, thawed to room temperature*
> *1/2 cup freshly grated Parmesan cheese*
> *1 cup grated mozzarella cheese*
> *1 cup thinly sliced onion*
> *2 pounds ripe, medium-size tomatoes, cut into 1/4-inch-thick slices*
> *1/4 teaspoon dried oregano*
> *1/4 teaspoon dried thyme*
> *salt and freshly ground black pepper to taste*

1. Preheat the oven to 375°F.

2. Brush a large cookie sheet with butter. Roll up one half of the stack of phyllo, rewrap it tightly in plastic, and put it back in the refrigerator until you need it. Using the remaining phyllo, take one sheet and place it on the cookie sheet. Butter it with your soft brush and melted butter. Add the next sheet, sprinkle with Parmesan cheese, and continue buttering and sprinkling with the Parmesan until you have seven layers in total. It is okay to overlap each layer to fit the cookie sheet. Crimp the edges around so you form an edge. Sprinkle the top layer with the grated mozzarella, sprinkle the onion slices over the tomato slices creating a grid of tomatoes about 1 1/2 inches apart. Season with the oregano, thyme, salt, and pepper.

3. Bake until golden brown, 45 to 50 minutes. Serve on a large tray or bread board, cutting squares with one tomato for each serving.

TOMATO PHYLLO PIZZA

CHICKEN FRICASSEE WITH PARSLEYED DUMPLINGS

CHICKEN FRICASSEE
WITH PARSLEYED DUMPLINGS

The chicken in this old-fashioned stew literally falls off the bone, the sauce around it is velvety and smooth, and the dumplings that float on top of it are filled with parsley and are like eating clouds. Some people think of creamed chicken as the ultimate comfort food—chicken fricassee beats creamed chicken by miles. One thing to remember is the importance of the timing of this dish. It is at its absolute best when it's hot, right from the oven.

For the dumplings

2 cups all-purpose flour
4 teaspoons baking powder
1 1/2 teaspoons salt
1/4 cup Crisco vegetable shortening
2/3 cup milk
1/4 cup minced fresh parsley leaves
2 large eggs, lightly beaten

For the fricassee

2 tablespoons vegetable oil
1/4 cup (1/2 stick) butter
one 6-pound chicken, cut into serving pieces
1 medium-size onion, stuck with 2 cloves
4 medium-size carrots, halved
bouquet garni (composed of 3 sprigs fresh parsley,
    2 celery tops, and 1 bay leaf wrapped
    together in cheesecloth)
7 cups chicken broth (canned is fine)

For the roux

3 tablespoons butter
3 tablespoons all-purpose flour
1/2 cup heavy cream
salt and freshly ground pepper to taste

continued

The dumpling dough can be made up to 1 day in advance and kept refrigerated, covered with plastic wrap.

Don't be put off by how messy the dumplings look on top of the chicken. The baking powder makes them puff up beautifully and even out.

Make sure your baking powder is freshly purchased, within the last 8 months.

1. To prepare the dumplings, in a medium-size bowl, combine the flour, baking powder, and salt. Cut in the shortening with a pastry cutter or two knives until the mixture resembles coarse meal. Add the milk, parsley, and beaten eggs, working the ingredients with a fork until the flour is just moistened and the mixture forms a soft ball. Work lightly and do not overmix. Set aside, covered with plastic wrap, or refrigerate, tightly wrapped, for up to 1 day.

2. To prepare the fricassee, heat the oil and butter together in a large, heavy skillet over medium-high heat until hot but not smoking. Place the chicken pieces in the skillet and cook until golden brown on all sides, about 15 minutes. Transfer the chicken to a large casserole dish fitted with a lid. Add the onion, carrots, and bouquet garni to the casserole dish. Add the chicken broth and bring to a boil over medium-high heat. Reduce the heat to low, cover, and simmer until the chicken is quite tender but not falling apart, about 1 hour.

3. Using a slotted spoon, transfer the chicken to a heatproof plate and cover with a sheet of aluminum foil. Set aside.

4. Pour the cooking liquid through a strainer and discard the onion and bouquet garni. Return the liquid to the casserole and keep warm over low heat.

5. To make the roux, melt the butter in a small saucepan over medium heat. Lower the heat and stir in the flour; cook until the mixture starts to brown, 3 to 4 minutes. Add the heavy cream and season with salt and pepper. Increase the heat under the chicken liquid to medium and whisk the roux into the chicken liquid. Reduce the heat to low and continue to whisk until it thickens to a velvety consistency. Stir with a wooden spoon until the roux thickens. Put the chicken back into the gravy.

6. To cook the dumplings, drop heaping tablespoons of the dumpling dough on top of the fricassee. Cover the fricassee and bring to a simmer over medium-high heat. Cook until the dumplings are puffed up and steamed, about 12 minutes. The fricassee can be kept in a warmed oven for up to 30 minutes.

BUTTER LETTUCE SALAD

I've called for butter lettuce because it is a springtime lettuce. If you can't get it, use Boston lettuce or another tender green. Either of my salad dressings (page 232) will work just fine.

> *2 heads butter lettuce*
> *¹/₂ cucumber, peeled and thinly sliced*
> *¹/₂ red onion, thinly sliced*
> *¹/₂ cup Ellen's Dressing of your choice*

1. Pick the very best and sweetest leaves from the lettuce, then wash and drain or spin-dry. Wrap the leaves loosely in paper towels until you use them, or put them directly into your salad bowl. Tear the large ones into manageable pieces. Add the cucumber and onion slices and cover with a clean, dry dish towel. Refrigerate.

2. To serve: Add the dressing and toss well to coat all the leaves. Serve immediately.

RHUBARB AND YOGURT PARFAITS

ELLEN'S TIPS

Trim off any leaves and discard them; I'm told that they are poisonous.

Rhubarb has a great deal of water in it, which will release during the cooking process. This helps cook the rhubarb to perfection.

Choose red or pink stalks because they are much prettier after cooking. The green ones taste the same but don't look as pretty.

Allow the rhubarb to get tender but not totally mushy. I know the rhubarb is done when it is just about to boil. I turn the heat off almost immediately after that point.

All you are doing here is stewing rhubarb with some sugar, which makes it nice and sweet, then serving it topped with plain yogurt in parfait glasses. Make the parfaits very pretty, if you like, by alternating the rhubarb and yogurt. If you have time, make up a batch of my Pie Crust Cookies (page 284). They go beautifully with the parfaits. You could also serve the stewed rhubarb over Home-made Vanilla Ice Cream (page 26), creating sundaes, which would be fancier and make a very good spring dessert, too.

> *12 medium-size stalks pink rhubarb,*
> *cut into 1-inch-thick slices*
> *1 cup sugar*
> *one 1-quart container plain yogurt*

Place the rhubarb and sugar in a large skillet and shake to distribute the sugar evenly. Cover the skillet and place over low heat. Cook, stirring several times to avoid burning the sugar. When the rhubarb is tender and soft, about 5 minutes, remove the skillet from the heat and let cool, uncovered. Transfer the rhubarb to a bowl and refrigerate, covered, for up to 3 days. Serve the rhubarb in large goblets or parfait glasses with a generous dollop of yogurt.

RHUBARB AND YOGURT PARFAITS

Easter Sunday Dinner

SALMON MOUSSE
ROAST BEEF WITH YORKSHIRE PUDDING
ASPARAGUS WITH CRUMBLED EGGS
BUTTERED CARROTS
GOLDEN BUNDT CAKE WITH CHOCOLATE LEAVES

Serves 6 to 8

We used to spend Easter Sunday with Mama Wright and Joe's family. His sisters and their group would always do a meal together in Oklahoma. Sometimes one or two of my kids would join us, but it was the Wrights' time to have us visit with them. There were always Easter egg hunts for the little ones and decorations as well. We miss seeing them now because Mama and Papa Wright have passed on, but it is still one of Joe's favorite holidays. We try to celebrate with a formal dinner with friends. Spring is Joe's favorite season, and Easter, for him, typifies all the budding new life of spring.

Because it is a special day, I make a special menu, and I decorate the house with vases of yellow tulips and purple iris so it says spring everywhere, inside and out. We eat in the dining room, where I set the table with a white damask tablecloth and napkins to match. On Easter, we always have asparagus and I serve it on plates that were given to us by my dear friend Soni. They are beautiful majolica plates in the shape of asparagus bunches and each one is different.

I keep them in the plate rack of the sideboard. On special occasions I take them down and serve asparagus on them. They're almost too pretty to eat on.

Something that I have done for years on Easter is decorate the table with eggs that Joe inherited from his father. They are made of semiprecious stones—agate, carnelian, and lapis lazuli. I place them randomly on the tablecloth with painted eggs, too. It's kind of fun and charming as well.

Serve with a claret, like a 1989 or 1995 St.-Emilion, or serve with a Pauillac.

SALMON MOUSSE

This recipe belongs to Richard De Combray, an old good friend, a writer, photographer, and bon vivant, who used to have wonderful parties at his home in New York. One night, while I was at a casual buffet dinner at his house, I was in the kitchen doing the dishes. A woman was helping me and we were chatting. We agreed it was better to be in the kitchen stacking the dishwasher than in the living room with all the other people making small talk. It turns out this woman was Lillian Hellman, the writer. I had no idea! Not long after that, she came to dinner at our apartment and asked that I play the piano for her. I did. I never play for anyone, but I played about an hour, and she listened. At the end, she said, "You should be spanked. If I could play the piano like that, I'd be so happy." The grass is always greener. I retorted with, "If I could write even a letter as well as you can, I would be happy."

This salmon mousse always makes me think of that night. It's easy to make and it tastes good. It can be made a day in advance.

ELLEN'S TIPS

There is one warning here that I ignored the first time I made it. I used a medium-size onion because I thought more would be better, but it wasn't. Use a small onion.

I love to use a curved fish mold for this mousse because it looks so good, but any attractive mold will do. In fact, I sometimes use three or four smaller molds on the platter.

> 1 envelope unflavored gelatin
> 2 tablespoons freshly squeezed lemon juice
> 1 small onion, quartered
> ½ cup boiling water
> salt and freshly ground black pepper to taste
> ½ cup mayonnaise
> ¼ teaspoon sweet paprika
> 2 teaspoons chopped fresh dill or ½ teaspoon
>   dried, plus extra for garnishing
> one 16-ounce can salmon, drained and
>   picked over for skin and bones
> 1 cup heavy cream
> oil for greasing the mold
> fresh dill, for garnish

1. Combine the gelatin, lemon juice, onion, boiling water, and salt and pepper in a blender. Blend until thoroughly combined, 40 seconds. Add the mayonnaise, paprika, dill, and salmon and blend, slowly adding the cream, until the mixture is smooth.

continued

Salmon Mousse

2. Lightly oil a 2-quart mold or individual molds and pour the mixture into the mold. Wrap well with plastic and refrigerate overnight. When ready to unmold, slip the mold into warm water for a few seconds and then invert it onto a plate. Sometimes it takes more than a few tries to unmold the mousse. Keep dipping it in the warm water until it loosens.

3. Decorate with fresh dill and serve.

ROAST BEEF WITH
YORKSHIRE PUDDING

This recipe is part mine and part my mother's. My mother made this dish very well and often; in fact, it was usually our Sunday midday lunch when we were growing up. The meat had the most wonderful aroma as it roasted because she used whole allspice in the pan to flavor it. Where that touch came from, I don't know. My mother's mother came from Germany and I suspect my mother learned it from her, and now my daughters have learned it from me.

Yorkshire pudding is what I like to serve with roast beef. My mother preferred roasted or mashed potatoes, and there is no doubt that they are delicious as well.

> 1 *standing rib roast of beef (5 to 6 pounds), about 3 ribs*
> 2 *tablespoons kosher salt*
> 2 *tablespoons whole allspice berries*
> 1 *cup beef broth (canned is fine)*
> 2 *teaspoons Wondra flour (quick-mixing flour for the gravy)*
> 1 *bunch watercress, for garnish*

1. Preheat the oven to 450°F.

2. Rub the meat generously with the salt. Place the roast on a rack in a roasting pan and sprinkle the allspice in the bottom of the pan. Roast for 30 minutes, then reduce the oven temperature to 350°F and roast until the meat is medium-rare, about another 60 minutes. If using a meat thermometer, it should read 140°F for medium-rare.

3. Remove the roast from the pan and transfer to a platter. Let the roast rest at room temperature for 15 minutes before carving. Pour off ½ cup drippings from the pan to use in the Yorkshire Pudding and set aside.

4. To make the gravy, take the roasting pan with its remaining juices and spices and put it over medium heat. Deglaze the pan with the beef broth and add the flour to the pan. Cook the gravy, scraping with a wooden spoon and stirring

To test meat for doneness, I use the finger test. I push the center of the roast with my finger. If the meat is hard and resistant, it's too well done. If it's soft and mushy, it's raw. If the meat is slightly resistant and somewhat firm, it's medium rare. This is not an exact science, but once you're familiar with the technique, it's very useful.

You can also deglaze the roasting pan with ¼ cup of red wine to add flavor to your gravy, if desired.

until it thickens. Add more broth or flour as necessary. Strain through a fine sieve and keep warm until serving.

5. Serve on a large platter garnished with watercress sprigs.

YORKSHIRE PUDDING

You must make this batter far enough ahead for it to get very cold. It's the difference between the temperature of the pan and the pudding that makes the pudding puff. It's magic.

> *2 cups sifted all-purpose flour*
> *1 teaspoon salt*
> *2 cups half-and-half*
> *4 large eggs*
> *½ cup roast drippings or canola oil (see Ellen's Tip)*

ELLEN'S TIP

The Yorkshire Pudding is much tastier when cooked in the drippings from the roast beef. If you have leftover bacon or goose grease, that works very well.

1. Place the flour, salt, half-and-half, and eggs in a large bowl and beat with an electric mixer on medium-high until very smooth. Cover and chill for at least 3 hours or preferably overnight.

2. Preheat the oven to 450°F. Put the drippings or canola oil in an 8-inch square glass baking dish and place in the oven until the fat starts smoking, 5 to 7 minutes.

3. Pour the *cold* batter into the dish and bake for 15 minutes. When the pudding has risen, reduce the oven temperature to 350°F and bake until golden brown and crisp, 15 to 20 minutes more. Cut into squares and serve around the roast.

ROAST BEEF WITH YORKSHIRE PUDDING AND
ASPARAGUS WITH CRUMBLED EGGS

ASPARAGUS
WITH CRUMBLED EGGS

ELLEN'S TIPS

The thing to remember here is 13 minutes—no more, no less—to cook the asparagus perfectly.

To keep the asparagus fresh before steaming, place them in a skillet and cover with cold water and several ice cubes.

Hard-boiled eggs take 10 minutes to cook starting with cold water. Peel them, and use only the yolks for this recipe.

If you can, always try to buy asparagus spears of more or less the same thickness. That way, they cook in the same amount of time. You can cook the asparagus ahead of time here, but wait to garnish it with the sieved egg yolk until just before serving.

36 medium-large (index-finger-thick) stalks asparagus,
trimmed of their woody bottoms
3 hard-boiled eggs, shelled, yolks only
½ cup Ellen's Dressing (page 232)

1. Put the asparagus in a large saucepan filled with cold water. Set your timer for 13 minutes. Cook, over medium heat, uncovered, until you can pierce the stems easily with a sharp knife. It should be exactly 13 minutes. Drain the asparagus, and place on a serving platter.

2. Pour the dressing over the asparagus and let them marinate for about 30 minutes before decorating with the egg yolks. Force the egg yolks through a fine sieve and sprinkle over the pretty green stalks just before serving.

ASPARAGUS WITH
CRUMBLED EGGS

BUTTERED CARROTS

The way a meal looks on a plate, the actual colors and how they come together, matters. Carrots are the perfect choice from that point of view for this meal. They taste very sweet and are really easy to prepare. You can use baby carrots, but only ones that are ultra-fresh; sometimes they don't pass that test in the markets. I prefer to peel my own.

> 8 carrots, sliced into 1-inch-thick rounds
> 6 cups cold water
> 1 teaspoon sugar
> 2 tablespoons butter
> 1 tablespoon chopped fresh parsley leaves

1. Place the carrots in a large saucepan filled with the water. Add the sugar and bring to a boil over high heat. Cook the carrots until soft enough to pierce with a sharp knife, about 10 minutes.

2. Drain, place in a serving bowl, and toss with the butter. Keep warm. Before serving, sprinkle with the fresh parsley.

ELLEN'S TIPS

I like curly parsley for a garnish.

You can cut the carrots on the diagonal, into about 3-inch pieces, for a change.

Carrots should not be crunchy (when cooked) like other vegetables.

GOLDEN BUNDT CAKE WITH CHOCOLATE LEAVES

I am not and never have been above using cake mix and instant pudding if the end justifies the means, and in this case it more than does. This is a sensationally moist and delectable cake. Guests who have had it—and loved it—are amazed that it starts with a mix. The mix is doctored and altered so that you don't even know that it's in there. Frosted with chocolate and decorated with chocolate leaves, this cake is one you can be proud of. It is one of the best.

ONE 10-INCH BUNDT CAKE

1 tablespoon Crisco, for the Bundt pan
2 tablespoons all-purpose flour for the Bundt pan
one 16-ounce package yellow cake mix
one 3-ounce package instant vanilla pudding
1/2 cup water
1/4 cup sweet sherry, port, or Madeira
1 teaspoon freshly grated nutmeg
4 large eggs
Chocolate Frosting (page 153)
Chocolate Leaves (page 153)

1. Preheat the oven to 350°F. Grease and flour a 10-inch Bundt pan. Knock out the excess flour.

2. Beat the cake mix with the instant pudding, water, sherry, nutmeg, and eggs using an electric mixer set on medium speed for at least 5 minutes. Increase the speed to high and mix for another 2 minutes.

3. Pour the batter into the prepared pan. Bake in the middle of the oven until golden brown and slightly pulling away from the sides of the pan, about 45 minutes.

4. Let cool for 30 minutes and loosen with a sharp knife until the cake inverts on a plate. Work slowly and it will come out well. When cool, frost with the Chocolate Frosting and decorate with the Chocolate Leaves.

CHOCOLATE FROSTING

This is a no-cook frosting that comes together very easily and tastes divine. It is not made with melted chocolate, but with unsweetened cocoa, which makes it a little less intense in flavor. I like that, especially since the cake is garnished with chocolate leaves.

MAKES 1 CUP

1/2 cup (1 stick) butter, at room temperature
one 16-ounce box confectioners' sugar
1 teaspoon pure vanilla extract
3 tablespoons unsweetened cocoa powder (Hershey's is fine)
3 tablespoons strong brewed coffee, cooled
3 tablespoons milk

Using a wooden spoon, beat the butter and sugar together in a medium-size bowl until smooth. Add the vanilla and cocoa powder. Slowly add the coffee and milk and mix together until it is smooth and creamy.

CHOCOLATE LEAVES

No one will believe that you made these chocolate leaves yourself. I learned how to do them many years ago from a fascinating woman, Stella Wilson, from South Africa, whom I met when I was living in California. Stella would just walk outside, pick some lemon leaves from her garden, and brush them with a chocolate mixture that is called a ganache. Then she would chill the leaves and peel the chocolate off. These leaves are lovely on Golden Bundt Cake or over ice cream.

MAKES 6 TO 8 LARGE LEAVES

4 ounces semi-sweet chocolate, chopped
2 ounces unsweetened chocolate, chopped
1/4 cup (1 stick) unsalted butter
10 to 12 lemon leaves or other firm, medium-size leaves
    (see Ellen's Tips, page 154), stems left on   *continued*

GOLDEN BUNDT CAKE WITH CHOCOLATE LEAVES

ELLEN'S TIPS

You will notice that I do not recommend an electric mixer for this frosting. If you use one, the frosting becomes too fluffy and isn't as pure a chocolate frosting.

You can make the frosting using either half coffee and half milk or all milk or all coffee. Using only coffee gives it the flavor of mocha. Using only milk makes for a richer chocolate frosting. It is important to add the liquid slowly to achieve the consistency you want. If you add all of the liquid at once, it will become too watery and won't spread well.

ELLEN'S TIPS

I melt my chocolate and butter in a glass measuring cup in the microwave until it is softened, 20 to 40 seconds.

If you opt to freeze the chocolate leaves with the green leaves still attached, let them thaw a bit before you peel them off. Otherwise, they will crack.

Work quickly or the heat of your hand will melt the chocolate and it will fall apart.

Lemon leaves are the best to use. If you use other leaves, make sure they are about the size of a plum. Anything smaller is difficult to work with.

You will need to use a soft pastry brush or a paint brush to make these leaves. Pastry brushes are available at housewares stores.

1. Place the chocolate and butter in the top of a double boiler over simmering water and melt slowly, stirring occasionally. Keep warm over low heat. The temperature should be about 70°F to brush on the leaves.

2. Gently brush the chocolate over the undersides of the leaves. Place the leaves on a baking sheet lined with a sheet of wax paper or aluminum foil. Allow the chocolate to harden at room temperature. Spread a second layer of chocolate on the leaves and again allow to harden. Two or three coats of chocolate are enough to make a good chocolate leaf. (The green leaf should be completely covered on the underside, but if the chocolate looks thin, three coats are necessary. If the chocolate is thick enough to show brush marks, it is too cold and can be heated up.) Transfer the leaves to the freezer until they are set.

3. In about 20 minutes, carefully pull off the chocolate leaf, starting by bending the green stem away from the chocolate. Do not touch them too long because the heat of your hand will melt the chocolate almost immediately. Use the blade of a small sharp knife to help you. Place the chocolate leaves back in the freezer lightly covered with plastic wrap until you decorate the cake and serve it. They will keep for 3 days.

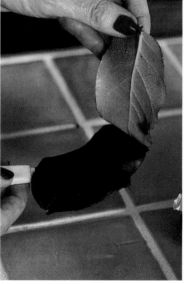

MAKING CHOCOLATE LEAVES

An Early Dinner al Fresco
with My Ex-Husband and Sarah

DEVILED EGGS FOR A NOSH
BANGED CHICKEN
STEWED TOMATOES WITH DUMPLINGS
ICEBERG WEDGES WITH BLUE CHEESE DRESSING
APRICOT SHERBET AND LACE COOKIES

Serves 6

Some people find it strange that I would be inviting my ex-husband and his wife to lunch. Joe and I don't think so. We enjoy each other's company and get along fine. And, anyway, Mitch and Sarah like good food. It's always fun to see how Mitch will rate my cooking on a scale of one to ten the next day, after he's had a chance to really mull the meal over. Knowing that, though, I don't deviate from my principles of easy and tasty, and I purposely keep the meal simple. If it's one of our warmer spring days, I serve it family-style on the terrace. I put out paisley napkins and cut whatever flowers are in bloom—maybe daffodils.

As you can see, the menu is very low key. You may wonder about a recipe called "Banged" Chicken (page 160), but don't. All "banged" means really is flattened. I first tasted this style of chicken in Florence many years ago at a little trattoria called Gilibar, and I've been making it the Gilibar way ever since. Although the chef cooked his chicken over a wood-burning grill, I pan-fry it. Either way, it is crunchy and delicious. The rest of the menu is simple too.

Serve this al fresco dinner with a slightly chilled Pinot Noir from Washington State, or with a cool Beaujolais.

DEVILED EGGS
FOR A NOSH

Deviled eggs, which I've always loved, were incredibly popular once, then faded a bit. I never stopped making them and still serve them with great appreciation. You're not meant to eat a lot of them; they really are "for a nosh." If you like capers, which I do, sprinkle a few on top of the filling. They make the eggs that much better.

6 large hard-boiled eggs, cooled
1 tablespoon mayonnaise
1 teaspoon prepared mustard
salt and freshly ground black pepper to taste
fresh parsley sprigs or capers, for garnish

Peel the eggs and cut them in half lengthwise. Remove the yolks without breaking the whites and put the yolks in a medium-size bowl. Add the mayonnaise and mustard and mash until smooth. Season and mix again. Put the mash in a pastry tube and pipe back into the white, or use a teaspoon to fill it. Decorate each half with a tiny parsley sprig or one or two capers.

ELLEN'S TIPS

To hard-boil eggs, put 1 tablespoon white vinegar with 2 quarts of water in a large saucepan. Carefully drop in the eggs and bring them to a boil. Turn off the heat and let the eggs sit for 10 minutes. Take them out to cool, or peel them immediately under cold running water.

You can sprinkle a bit of paprika for decoration on top of the mashed yolks before garnishing with a caper or a sprig of parsley.

You may use 2 teaspoons of Colman's dry mustard in place of the ordinary prepared mustard if you'd like some zing. Try some each way and see which you like best.

BANGED CHICKEN

ELLEN'S TIPS

I suggest you flatten the chicken in advance so that you will spare your guests the noise. Rest assured, this dish is worth the effort.

Serve with a lemon wedge for garnish.

You can put a piece of aluminum foil in between the chicken and the weight to keep them both clean.

There are a lot of reasons to make Banged Chicken and not just for its name, which does prove to be something of a conversation piece. You flatten the breasts—bones still in—by pounding them with the bottom of a heavy skillet. (If you're feeling particularly aggressive, this is very therapeutic!) The pounding actually tenderizes the meat; breaking the bones releases flavor into the meat and evens the pieces out so that they cook uniformly. The result is juicy, tender chicken breasts, with a wonderful taste. Be sure that you allow your skillet to get very hot.

3 whole bone-in chicken breasts (about 3 pounds), halved
1 tablespoon dried thyme
1 tablespoon dried rosemary
kosher salt

1. Flatten the chicken breasts by placing them one at a time into a resealable plastic bag. Bang with a heavy skillet or meat mallet. The bones of the chicken will break and the pieces should be flattened until they are ½ inch thick. Season the chicken pieces on both sides generously with the dried herbs and set aside. This seasoning acts like a marinade and can be done a few hours in advance. Refrigerate the chicken until ready to cook.

2. Sprinkle 1 tablespoon salt on a hot cast-iron skillet set over medium-high heat. Place the chicken pieces in the skillet, underside down, and weight them down with a full tea kettle, a heavy pot, or similar object. Brown the pieces for about 8 minutes, until well browned. Turn the chicken over, adding more salt to the skillet. Weight the chicken down again, browning until done. Serve immediately.

BANGED CHICKEN AND
STEWED TOMATOES WITH DUMPLINGS

STEWED TOMATOES
WITH DUMPLINGS

ELLEN'S TIPS

*You can make the dough
for the dumplings 1 day
in advance.*

*If you reheat this dish, add
¼ cup water to the toma-
toes because they tend
to get dry.*

This is a simple and really flavorful vegetable side dish, and whenever you serve it, you can forgo potatoes or bread. I like these tomatoes, in particular, with the Banged Chicken, although they also go very well with grilled fish, steak, or chops. They are simple and elegant.

For the sauce

one 28-ounce can whole peeled tomatoes in their juice
1 medium-size onion, grated
1 teaspoon butter
2 teaspoons light brown sugar
1 teaspoon fennel seeds

For the dumplings

1 cup all-purpose flour
2 teaspoons baking powder
1 tablespoon vegetable shortening
½ cup milk

1. Bring the tomatoes, onion, butter, sugar, and fennel seeds to a boil in a medium-size saucepan over medium-high heat. Simmer for 5 to 6 minutes. Keep warm.

2. In a large bowl, combine the flour and baking powder. Using a pastry cutter or two knives, cut in the shortening until the mixture resembles coarse meal. Add the milk, mixing gently with a fork so as not to overmix the dough. You can also do this in a food processor, pulsing to combine the dough quickly.

3. Bring the tomato liquid back to a simmer over medium heat. Let the dough stand a few minutes and then drop the dough, 1 tablespoon at a time, into the simmering tomato mixture. Cover and cook until the dumplings are large and fluffy, about 12 minutes. Serve with any meat, chicken, or fish dish.

ICEBERG WEDGES
WITH BLUE CHEESE DRESSING

Iceberg lettuce, the only lettuce anyone could get at the supermarket for years on end, also plummeted in popularity a while back—in the same way poor old deviled eggs did. However, it never fell out of favor with me. I've always liked it. Cold iceberg is the crunchiest and the sweetest of all the lettuces. Cut a large head into big wedges, stir some crumbled blue cheese or Gorgonzola into one of my dressings (page 232) and spoon lots of the dressing on top of the iceberg. Serve the salad with a fork and knife.

APRICOT SHERBET

Thirty years ago, when I had young kids and no time to cook, I was given this recipe by my sister-in-law Joyce. It is easy to make—only three ingredients—and happens to be delicious. It's also very reassuring to know that you have a dessert in the freezer, ready to serve any time you need one. Apricot sherbet is especially refreshing for dessert, and it pairs beautifully with one of my all-time favorite cookies—Lace Cookies (page 166). Please trust me and have a pitcher of cold heavy cream to serve on top of the sherbet. It is naughty but good.

> *two 36-ounce jars apricot preserves*
> *two 8-ounce cans pitted apricots, not drained*
> *½ cup freshly squeezed lemon juice*
> *heavy cream, for serving*

Warm the preserves in a small saucepan over medium heat. Strain and discard what won't go through the strainer. Set aside. Puree the pitted apricots with the lemon juice until smooth. Add the jam and pulse to combine. Pour the mixture into a plastic container and chill in the freezer for at least 24 hours. Serve with a pitcher of heavy cream alongside the sherbet.

APRICOT SHERBET AND
LACE COOKIES

This can be made up to 2 weeks ahead of time.

I like to serve this sherbet in wineglasses or pretty little bowls, drizzled lightly with the cream.

LACE COOKIES

These are special cookies—so lacy you can see right through them. There is barely any flour in the batter, which means the cookies hold together because of the sugar, butter, and almonds. They are made to be served with sherbet or ice cream. My daughter Claudia, mother of two small children, makes these faster and better than I do. She's undaunted when it comes to baking, and you should be, too. Do yourself a favor by first reading my Tips; they'll prove useful, especially if it is the first time you've ever made these lacy treats.

MAKES ABOUT 40 COOKIES

1/2 cup (1 stick) butter, softened,
   plus extra for the cookie sheet
2 tablespoons all-purpose flour,
   plus extra for the cookie sheet
1/2 cup sugar
1 cup ground almonds
2 tablespoons milk

1. Preheat the oven to 350°F.

2. Grease and flour a cookie sheet. Tap out any excess flour. In a large bowl, mix all the ingredients together with a fork until combined. Pour the batter onto the cookie sheet 1½ teaspoons at a time.

3. Bake until the cookies are golden brown, 8 to 10 minutes. Remove the cookie sheet from the oven, cool for 1 minute, then remove the cookies with a spatula while they are still warm and malleable. Grease and flour the cookie sheet for each batch of cookies. Cool the cookies completely on a rack before storing in a tin.

This batter is thin and buttery and it spreads out very quickly on the cookie sheet. Leave 1 1/2 inches in between each cookie.

Don't forget to grease and flour the cookie sheet each time you prepare to bake another batch.

The most important thing to remember is when the cookies are golden brown like toffee, immediately remove them from the oven and let them cool about 60 seconds. Quickly transfer them to a rack or plate while they are still soft. It is important to work quickly because the cookies harden within a few minutes and become brittle and difficult to remove from the cookie sheet.

Outdoor Lunch
Under the Crabapple Tree

CHICKEN LIVER PÂTÉ WITH CORNICHONS
ASPARAGUS QUICHE
TOMATO ASPIC WITH PINEAPPLE SAUCE
CHOCOLATE SPONGE CAKE

Serves 6

When the crabapple tree blooms in our garden, I either want to see someone married under its blossoms or I want to be under that fluffy pink umbrella having a delicious lunch with friends. The blossoms last for such a short time that to hesitate is to miss out on the magic of the sight. So when the tree is in bloom, I move a small bistro table under its branches. I set it with simple white plates and pink and purple napkins, and we bring the whole meal out on a tray.

This menu is so simple to prepare and all of it can be made in advance. That is why it is a standby for me.

We have the pâté at the table, or better yet, in the living room at the coffee table with a glass of crisp cold Pinot Grigio or a glass of lemonade. Then we move outside to serve the quiche and salad with a white Burgundy or a cold Montrachet. We might take a stroll before dessert through our perfectly weeded garden, which in no time will be yielding dahlias by the armful.

Lunch in the country, unlike dinner, can be as relaxed as you want to make it. If you don't have a crabapple tree, any pretty tree will do. If you don't have a tree, an umbrella will work. The point is to be outside, with good company and good food. It's spring.

CHICKEN LIVER PÂTÉ
WITH CORNICHONS

M y father's parents lived across the street from us when I was growing up. My Grandma Bessie was a quiet, sweet Russian woman who spoke almost no English. I remember going to visit her many an afternoon and standing beside her at the kitchen table—I was barely as tall as the table—watching her bake. She loved to bake; sweet rolls and pinwheels were her specialty, and she also made this pâté, which I have never forgotten. It's rich and smooth and delicious and I never knew what she called it in Russian. I do remember her always giving me a piece of bread with the pâté on it and her saying, "Eat it, dahlink, it's good for you!" I am sure a few doctors would disagree with that today, but anything that good in small doses can't be all bad. The cornichons are my addition.

ELLEN'S TIP

The pâté can be frozen for up to 2 weeks if tightly wrapped.

1 cup (2 sticks) butter, at room temperature
½ cup chopped onion
2 tablespoons chopped shallots
1 tart apple, cored, peeled, and chopped
1 pound chicken livers, trimmed of membranes
¼ cup Calvados or applejack brandy, warmed
2 to 4 tablespoons heavy cream, to your taste
1 teaspoon freshly squeezed lemon juice
1½ teaspoons salt
¼ teaspoon freshly ground black pepper
1 cup cornichon pickles

1. Melt 3 tablespoons of the butter in a medium-size skillet over medium heat. Add the onion, shallots, and apple and cook, stirring, until softened. Set aside.

2. Melt 3 more tablespoons of the butter in a large skillet over medium heat and cook the chicken livers until medium cooked, about 7 minutes, turning them several times. Add the warmed Calvados or applejack and carefully light it with a long match, averting your face and keeping long hair and hanging sleeves out of the way. Let it flame out by itself.

3. Place the apple mixture and chicken livers in a food processor and process until smooth, adding the heavy cream a little at a time to achieve the consistency of

sour cream. Add $\frac{1}{2}$ cup of the butter and process again until smooth. Mix in the lemon juice, salt, and pepper.

4. Melt the remaining 2 tablespoons of butter in a small saucepan. Spoon the pâté into a dish or container and top with the melted butter to preserve the color of the pâté. You will scrape this butter off when you serve it. Wrap tightly and refrigerate overnight. Serve with toast squares, your favorite cracker, and the cornichons, which make a lovely accompaniment.

ASPARAGUS QUICHE

In 1961, I had the privilege of seeing Julia Child demonstrate this recipe at the San Francisco Legion of Honor Museum. She is the best at demystifying difficult or scary recipes. She taught the basics for making the quiche shell and she also showed the French way of preparing asparagus. I enjoyed meeting her many years later in Washington at a dear friend's home. Although this recipe looks long and complicated, it's really very easy.

MAKES ONE 9-INCH QUICHE

For the crust

1½ cups Wondra flour (quick-mixing flour
    for sauces and gravies)
½ cup (1 stick) butter, chilled and cut into pieces
3 tablespoons vegetable shortening
⅓ cup ice water
½ teaspoon salt

For the filling

3 large eggs
1¼ cups heavy cream
½ teaspoon salt
¼ cup chopped fresh parsley leaves
freshly ground white pepper to taste
7 to 8 stalks asparagus, trimmed of any woody bottoms
3 tablespoons butter
freshly ground black pepper to taste
½ cup freshly grated Gruyère cheese (Cheddar or
    Monterey Jack can also be used)

1. To make the crust, place the flour in a large bowl and, using two knives or a pastry cutter, cut the butter and vegetable shortening into the mixture until it resembles coarse meal. Add the ice water and salt and mix until the dough comes together. Form the dough into a ball. Wrap in wax paper and refrigerate for 2 hours.

continued

Next spread: **ASPARAGUS QUICHE AND TOMATO ASPIC WITH PINEAPPLE SAUCE**

Make sure the asparagus you use is green and tender. Do not use any woody bottoms.

Other vegetables could be used instead: broccoli, zucchini, mushrooms, onions, or tomatoes. You can also jazz up the flavor with herbs such as basil, oregano, thyme, or sage.

The crust can be made in a food processor by pulsing the ingredients quickly.

Sliced scallions or chopped chives can be substituted for parsley.

2. Preheat the oven to 425°F. Roll out the pastry about ¼ inch thick and fit it into a 9-inch quiche pan. Refrigerate for 1 hour. Prick the bottom of the dough liberally with a fork. Place another smaller pan inside to help set the sides while baking, or place a sheet of wax paper or parchment paper in the shell and fill with beans, rice, or pie weights.

3. Bake until the crust begins to feel firm, 5 to 7 minutes. Remove the inside pan (or weights) and return the crust to the oven. In about 2 minutes, use a fork to prick the crust, which will be lightly browned and puffed up. Remove the crust from the oven and set aside on a wire rack to cool slightly. Don't turn off the oven.

4. Meanwhile, to make the filling, mix the eggs, cream, salt, herbs, and white pepper together in a medium-size bowl with a fork and chill at least 30 minutes, or cover tightly, and refrigerate for up to 1 day.

5. Pour one third of the egg mixture into the partially baked quiche crust. Bake until the filling begins to set, about 10 minutes.

6. Meanwhile, cut the asparagus stalks in half. Heat 2 tablespoons of the butter over medium heat in a medium-size skillet. Cook the pieces of asparagus until tender, 4 to 6 minutes. The tips will cook faster than the bottoms, so remove them first. Season with the salt and black pepper and arrange in the quiche pan in a pretty pattern, like the spokes of a wheel. Pour the rest of the egg mixture over the asparagus. Sprinkle with the Gruyère cheese and dot with the remaining 1 tablespoon butter. Bake until puffed and brown, about 30 minutes. Serve hot or at room temperature.

TOMATO ASPIC WITH
PINEAPPLE SAUCE

This recipe is absolutely unique. It comes from Ann Wright, who was a good cook. She never told me if she invented this recipe or where she got it. What sets it apart is the pineapple sauce. You wouldn't think that tomatoes and pineapple would go together, but they do. I like to have a plate of this with crisp lettuce, topped with sauce, and some of my Cheese Straws (page 17) or Puff Pastry Sticks (page 115) for lunch.

For the aspic

one 3-ounce package lemon Jell-O
1 cup boiling water
3/4 cup stewed tomatoes or canned plum tomatoes,
    broken up
1/2 small onion, grated or finely minced to yield
    1 tablespoon pulp (see Ellen's Tips)
1/4 cup tomato puree
1/4 cup tomato juice
oil for greasing the mold

For the sauce

1 tablespoon freshly squeezed lemon juice
1/2 cup mayonnaise
1 tablespoon pineapple juice
1/2 cup crushed pineapple (canned is best), drained

1. In a large bowl, dissolve the Jell-O in the boiling water, stirring for a minute. Add the tomatoes, onion, tomato puree, and tomato juice and mix until the aspic is well combined. Pour the mixture into a lightly greased 1-quart mold or 8-inch square glass dish. Refrigerate, lightly covered, overnight. To remove from the mold, briefly* dip it into a bowl of hot water and unmold onto a chilled plate.

2. To make the sauce, in a small bowl, whisk together the lemon juice, mayonnaise, and pineapple juice. Add the crushed pineapple and stir lightly with a fork. Cover with plastic wrap and serve at room temperature with the aspic.

* *"Briefly" means about 10 seconds. If the aspic doesn't come out of the mold the first time, dip it again for 5 seconds. Have patience.*

CHOCOLATE SPONGE CAKE

I f you love chocolate cake the way most people do, you know that it comes in all different textures and flavors. This batter was passed down from someone's southern housekeeper many moons ago and is a winner. It contains 1 cup of boiling water, which is not a typical ingredient in chocolate cake batters. The water serves its purpose because the texture of this cake is moist and light and takes beautifully to the Mocha Frosting. Sponge cakes are meant to be light, and I think this one is perfect for spring.

MAKES ONE 8-INCH SQUARE CAKE

oil for greasing the baking dish
2 cups all-purpose flour, plus extra for the baking dish
2 cups sugar
1 level teaspoon baking soda
1/2 teaspoon salt
1/2 cup (1 stick) unsalted butter
1/4 cup unsweetened cocoa powder (Hershey's is fine)
2 large eggs
1/2 cup buttermilk (see Ellen's Tips)
1 cup boiling water
Mocha Frosting (recipe follows)

1. Preheat the oven to 300°F. Grease and flour an 8-inch square glass baking dish. Set aside.

2. Mix the flour, sugar, baking soda, and salt together in a medium-size bowl. Set aside. In a small saucepan, melt the butter with the cocoa over low heat, stirring them together well. Pour the chocolate mixture into a medium-size bowl and mix in the eggs until well combined. Using a wooden spoon or an electric mixer on medium, beat in the dry ingredients, alternating with the buttermilk. Beat until smooth. Add the boiling water and mix well until the batter is smooth and thin. Pour the batter into the prepared baking dish.

3. Bake in the center of the oven until a toothpick inserted in the center of the cake comes out clean, 45 to 55 minutes. Remove from the oven and let cool completely. Frost with Mocha Frosting.

ELLEN'S TIPS

To make buttermilk, place 2 teaspoons white vinegar and 1 cup whole milk in a jar. Cover the jar and shake to mix well. Let the mixture sit at room temperature for 30 minutes until it begins to clot. Presto . . . buttermilk!

Store baking soda in the fridge and it will only keep for up to 6 months.

This batter will look "soupy." Don't worry— it's supposed to.

MOCHA FROSTING

¼ cup (½ stick) butter
2 ounces semi-sweet chocolate
2 cups confectioners' sugar
pinch of ground cinnamon
2 tablespoons strong brewed coffee, cooled
2 tablespoons milk

Melt the butter and chocolate together in a small saucepan over low heat or in the microwave, about 40 seconds. Slowly add the sugar, cinnamon, coffee, and milk, mixing until the mixture is smooth and not too thin. Cool and spread on the cooled cake. If you are in a hurry, refrigerate the frosting for 15 minutes before frosting the cake. The frosting can be made 3 days in advance and kept refrigerated. Bring to room temperature before using.

Surprise Birthday Dinner for Maureen

CRUDITÉS WITH CURRY DIP

ROSEMARY-MARINATED LAMB CHOPS
WITH APRICOT CHUTNEY

SPINACH, ENDIVE, AND WATERCRESS SALAD

SHORT-CIRCUIT CORN BREAD

SALLY'S CRUNCHY ALMOND CHEESECAKE

Serves 6 to 8

Maureen Cogan and I grew up together in Boston, and as little seven-year-old girls and best friends, we loved to play together. When Maureen's birthday rolled around this year, I invited only a few of her dearest friends to celebrate, those people whom she loves best. As anyone who has ever planned a surprise party knows, the logistics can be a little tricky. Joe, Maureen's husband, and I managed to work it out, convincing Maureen that just the four of us were going to have a very relaxed brisket dinner in the kitchen in Bridgehampton. By the time they arrived, our guests had, too, and no one was more surprised than Maureen!

It was a very simple menu, really easy to prepare and filled with a variety of flavors from course to course. I usually serve this meal with an Italian Brunello or a good Barolo. As party decorations, I had made copies of photographs of Maureen through the years and mounted each one on different colored construction paper, then folded them like invitations and tucked them between the tines of the forks around the table. There were descriptions on each photo—comments on how short her bangs were or how sweet sixteen wasn't—all sorts of choice tidbits and remarks. A birthday is not a birthday

without a cake, and Sally's Crunchy Almond Cheesecake (page 189) proved to be the perfect note on which to end. I garnished the top of it with one large purple orchid. The tablecloth was a Pierre Deux fabric in yellow and burgundy, and it all worked beautifully together, right down to the small bouquets of yellow tulips and beautiful dried cranberries on the stem. We drank toasts with dessert to her ongoing good looks and many more years of reliable health. Maureen could not stop repeating how happy she was.

CURRY DIP

½ cup mayonnaise
½ cup sour cream
1 tablespoon curry powder (see Ellen's Tip)
1 tablespoon freshly squeezed lemon juice
2 teaspoons chopped fresh cilantro leaves, for garnish

Combine the mayonnaise, sour cream, curry powder, and lemon juice in a medium-size bowl and mix with a fork until smooth. Chill well. Garnish with chopped cilantro leaves just before serving.

ELLEN'S TIP

Curry powder is made from at least three different spices. For 1 tablespoon combine:

1 teaspoon ground cumin
1 teaspoon ground coriander
1 teaspoon ground turmeric

Make sure it is fresh—within 3 months.

ROSEMARY-MARINATED
LAMB CHOPS WITH
APRICOT CHUTNEY

ELLEN'S TIP

*Have a hot grill or broiler
ready to do these chops so
that they are really brown
on the outside and medium
pink on the inside. Noth-
ing is worse than over- or
undercooked lamb.*

When I lived in San Francisco, I once asked a Japanese caterer to help me prepare hors d'oeuvres for a big cocktail party I was giving for friends. She made these lamb chops that night and I have never forgotten the taste of them or how she handled her perfectly sharpened knives, all arranged in her special carrying case. She brought her own fresh rosemary and other important ingredients. Those were the best lamb chops I had ever tasted, and I have reconstructed the recipe here—as close as I could. The apricot chutney is a key addition.

> *1 cup dry red wine*
> *1 tablespoon balsamic vinegar*
> *3 tablespoons fresh rosemary needles, finely chopped*
> *1 teaspoon sugar*
> *2 cloves garlic, crushed to a paste*
> *1 tablespoon sesame oil*
> *16 rib lamb chops*
> *Apricot Chutney (page 184), for serving*

1. In a small saucepan over low heat, cook the wine along with the vinegar, chopped rosemary, sugar, garlic, and sesame oil for 2 to 3 minutes until the herbs release their flavors. Remove from the stove and set aside to cool.

2. Place the chops in a shallow glass dish, pour the marinade over the chops, and let them marinate for 1 hour at room temperature, turning them from time to time to flavor the chops evenly.

3. Preheat the broiler and broil the chops until really nicely brown on the outside and pink inside, about 3 to 4 minutes per side. Serve with Apricot Chutney.

ROSEMARY-MARINATED LAMB CHOPS WITH APRICOT CHUTNEY
AND SPINACH, ENDIVE, AND WATERCRESS SALAD

APRICOT CHUTNEY

The only thing that can be a disaster here is if you burn the chutney while it is cooking. Even in a heavy casserole or cast-iron pan, it is a potential problem. The way to avoid this is to keep an eye on the chutney while it cooks and stir it often.

Make this condiment one day when you have some free time, and store it in a tightly covered crock in the fridge. I try to have it on hand in my fridge for lamb chops or hamburgers. It goes so well with so many things, even eggs. It keeps for 6 to 8 weeks.

I learned this recipe more than fifteen years ago when I took an Indian cooking class with Madhur Jaffrey, a superb teacher and wonderful Indian cook. The chutney is hot and sweet at the same time, and great with chops, meats, chicken, and fish. It keeps beautifully in the fridge and is a little like having a special mustard on hand, whenever you want to use it.

MAKES 2 CUPS

1 pound dried apricots
4 cups boiling water
8 large cloves garlic
one 2-inch piece fresh ginger, peeled and finely chopped
1½ cups red wine vinegar
2 cups sugar
¼ teaspoon salt
½ teaspoon cayenne pepper
¾ cup golden raisins

1. Cut the apricots into halves and soak them in the boiling water for 2 hours, covered. Drain the water and set them aside.

2. Place the garlic, ginger, and vinegar in the bowl of a food processor. Pulse until the mixture is almost a paste. Transfer the garlic mixture and the apricots to a large, heavy pot and cook over medium-low heat, adding the sugar, salt, and cayenne. Cook until the chutney is thickened and the apricots are very soft, about 45 minutes to an hour, stirring often with a wooden spoon so the sugar does not burn on the bottom. Add the raisins for the last 20 minutes of cooking. Let the chutney cool before serving. It can be served at room temperature or cold.

Spinach, Endive, and Watercress Salad

A combination of greens, all different colors, makes this the perfect salad to serve with the lamb chops and chutney. Tender baby spinach leaves are best, and remember to stem the watercress. Endive is a delicious lettuce and balances the tastes beautifully. I suggest my favorite vinaigrette, Ellen's Dressing (page 232); either variation is good.

> *one 12-ounce bag spinach*
> *2 Belgian endive*
> *1 medium-size bunch watercress*
> *½ cup dressing of your choice, plus extra if needed*

1. Wash the spinach in cold water several times to rid the leaves of sand. Even if it is prewashed, you should wash it again. Stem the leaves. Spin or pat it dry and place in a salad bowl.

2. Core the endive and split it lengthwise into quarters. Add to the salad bowl.

3. Stem the watercress and wash it as well. Spin or pat it dry and add to the bowl. Chill the greens for up to 2 hours, covered with a clean kitchen towel. Before serving, pour ½ cup of the dressing over the leaves and toss well to coat each leaf. Add more dressing if needed.

SHORT-CIRCUIT
CORN BREAD

This is a deliciously moist corn bread, and so many of them are not. I figured out the recipe years ago when I was trying to cut down on the preparation time. Starting with a corn bread mix gave me a good base, and the added ingredients really enhanced the perfection of the corn bread. Serve the bread warm with butter on the table for those who want it.

> *one 8-ounce package corn bread mix (I use Aunt Jemima or Dromedary)*
> *2 large eggs*
> *1 cup heavy cream*
> *¼ cup (½ stick) butter, melted, plus extra for the baking dish*
> *1 cup corn kernels, fresh or frozen and thawed*
> *3 tablespoons seeded and chopped chiles (canned are fine)*
> *¾ cup grated Monterey Jack cheese*

1. Preheat the oven to 375°F.

2. In a large bowl, mix the corn bread mix, eggs, and heavy cream together with an electric mixer on medium speed until smooth, about 3 minutes. Add the melted butter and mix again. Add the corn, chiles, and cheese and stir with a wooden spoon until mixed thoroughly.

3. Pour the batter into a buttered 8-inch square glass baking dish and bake until a sharp knife comes out clean, 30 to 35 minutes. Serve hot.

ELLEN'S TIPS

The canned chiles are mild and the ones in the jar are very hot, so be careful that you taste what you use.

Do not overbake the corn bread because the thing about this recipe is its moist texture.

SALLY'S CRUNCHY ALMOND CHEESECAKE

I love to make desserts—not so much to eat them, but to actually make them. You get to watch something grow and take shape, to build ingredients into something beautiful.

As cheesecakes go, this one is really a beauty. The recipe comes to me from a very special friend in San Francisco, Sally Gilbert. The first time I made Sally's cake, I chilled it and didn't bake it! I was young at the time and not up on cheesecakes, to say the least. But even at that, it tasted good. See if you don't think it's one of the best cheesecakes you've ever tasted.

MAKES ONE 9-INCH CAKE

For the crust

2¾ cups graham cracker crumbs (2 wrapped
    packages in a 16-ounce box)
⅓ cup very coarsely chopped blanched almonds
1 teaspoon pure vanilla extract
1 teaspoon pure almond extract (optional)
½ teaspoon ground cinnamon
1 tablespoon sugar
½ cup (1 stick) unsalted butter, melted

For the filling

3 large eggs, well beaten (see Ellen's Tips)
two 8-ounce packages cream cheese,
    at room temperature
1 cup granulated sugar
2 teaspoons pure vanilla extract
¼ teaspoon salt
3 cups sour cream

1. Preheat the oven to 375°F.

2. In a food processor, combine all of the crust ingredients and process until well combined. Press the mixture evenly (see Ellen's Tips) into the bottom and sides

ELLEN'S TIPS

When you press the crust into the springform pan, use your knuckles to press the crumbs down into place. The rounded bottom of a measuring cup is also a very good tool to press the crust into shape. You won't be able to get the sides as thick as the bottom. They'll be about ⅛ inch thick.

Take the cream cheese out ahead of time to soften it.

The eggs should also be at room temperature; they will produce more volume when beaten, which in turn produces a higher cake.

The almonds must be chopped into coarse pieces. I use blanched almonds. They are the secret to this great-tasting crust.

I leave out the almond extract because I don't like it. I add ½ teaspoon more of vanilla extract.

To hold the oven door
ajar, fold a pot holder
several times to allow
about a 3- to 4-inch space
for air to cool the cheese-
cake slowly.

of a 9-inch springform pan, about $\frac{1}{2}$ inch thick. Set aside in the refrigerator for at least 30 minutes.

3. In a large bowl, combine all the filling ingredients except the sour cream. Stir in the sour cream. Pour the batter into the prepared pan and bake until the top is brown, about 45 minutes. Turn off the oven and let cool about 15 minutes with the oven door ajar, then take it out and let it cool completely.

4. Remove the sides of the springform pan, cover the cheesecake with plastic wrap, and chill for at least 6 hours before serving.

Lunch After
the Potatohampton 10K

CRUDITÉS WITH YOGURT AND
BLUE CHEESE DIP
LILLIAN'S BAKED STEAK
POTATO PIE SOUTH AFRICAN STYLE
ENDIVE AND MANDARIN ORANGE SALAD
AUNT SADYE'S BROWNIES

Serves 8

It's finally Memorial Day weekend, the first big weekend of the summer, and the whole South Fork, from Westhampton to Montauk, is very busy. Unofficially and overnight, spring has changed to summer, and nothing is the same. There are cars everywhere and people are pouring out of the city in droves. In the village, you might have a problem finding a parking space. Too bad if you're delayed in going to the Candy Kitchen for the paper. The *New York Times* is sold out before ten A.M. It's nutty and a little electrifying. The season has begun.

Competing with the picnics and parties and barbecues that mark the start of this 3-day weekend is the Potatohampton 10K, an annual event. The race has a very low-key, hometown, and neighborly feel to it. The 6-mile route takes the runners around the potato fields of Bridgehampton and its environs. Over the years we have known a lot of the runners and have stood on the sidelines cheering them on. The Potatohampton race marks Memorial Day for us.

We like to serve a nice big lunch for runners and nonrunners that day. It is a good excuse to get together but also a way of applauding those who finished the race. I am not quite ready for outdoor grilling and so I do this menu indoors. Baked steak is something I learned how to prepare from a dear friend, Lillian Jankelson, when I lived in San Francisco.

Steak goes with potatoes and you'll want to make this potato pie even if all you've done is sit by the pool all day. And Aunt Sadye's Brownies (page 201) just might be the best and simplest brownies I've ever made. Serve lemonade, iced tea, and maybe some Gatorade for the runners. After all is said and done, you can work up quite a thirst watching other people run. If wine is desired, try a slightly chilled Beaujolais.

CRUDITÉS WITH YOGURT AND BLUE CHEESE DIP

Here is a recipe for basic crudités that serves 6 to 8 people. Feel free to add and subtract any veggies to suit your tastes.

1 cup cauliflower florets
1 cup broccoli florets
1 small cucumber, peeled and sliced into spears
3 medium-size carrots, cut into sticks
1 yellow or red bell pepper, seeded and cut into wedges
6 radishes, trimmed
Yogurt and Blue Cheese Dip (recipe follows)

Prepare the vegetables and keep them fresh in a serving dish covered lightly with a cool, damp towel. Refrigerate up to 1 hour before serving. Serve with the dip.

YOGURT AND BLUE CHEESE DIP

This is a great low-fat dressing for salads or used as a dip for vegetables. It's tasty enough even when you are not on a diet.

MAKES 1 CUP

1 cup plain yogurt (low-fat is optional)
1/2 cup crumbled blue cheese
2 teaspoons white vinegar
1/4 teaspoon freshly ground black pepper
2 tablespoons chopped fresh chives

In the bowl of a food processor, place the yogurt, blue cheese, vinegar, and pepper and pulse until smooth. Refrigerate, covered, up to 2 days or serve immediately. Place in a small serving bowl and garnish with the chopped chives.

LILLIAN'S BAKED STEAK

ELLEN'S TIP

If you don't have an instant-read thermometer, you can test the doneness of the meat by doing the "finger test." If, when pressing on the meat with your finger, it feels very soft and has little resistance, it's not cooked enough. When the meat feels somewhat firm and has some resistance, it's medium-rare to medium. If the meat is very firm, it's well done. Obviously, this is not an exact science.

Lillian Jankelson is one of my oldest friends and was an inspirational teacher and a mentor to me when I was first learning about interior design. Lillian taught me about restraint, which is a very difficult thing to teach. Like my father, who had great style, and my mother, who has good taste, Lillian knew when enough was enough. She said it was instinct. This steak recipe has the balance that Lillian understood. It's unique and proves that Porterhouse or T-bone steaks don't always have to be grilled.

one 2½-inch-thick T-bone or Porterhouse steak (about 3 pounds)
1 lemon, seeded and sliced
1 green bell pepper, seeded and sliced into ¼-inch-thick rings
1 large onion, sliced into ¼-inch-thick rings
1 cup ketchup
2 tablespoons Worcestershire sauce

1. Preheat the oven to 400°F.

2. Place the steak in a glass baking dish large enough to comfortably hold it. Arrange alternating slices of lemon, bell pepper, and onion over the meat. In a small bowl, combine the ketchup and Worcestershire. Pour the mixture over the meat. Bake until an instant-read thermometer reads 140°F for medium rare, 45 to 55 minutes.

3. To serve the steak, let it rest about 15 minutes before you carve it. Carefully move the lemon, peppers, and onions to one side. Slice the meat and garnish with the vegetables.

LILLIAN'S BAKED STEAK
AND POTATO PIE SOUTH AFRICAN STYLE

POTATO PIE
SOUTH AFRICAN STYLE

ELLEN'S TIPS

If you have a square or rectangular dish that is at least 3 inches deep, it is fine to use.

The dough can be made and kept in a ball 2 to 4 days in advance. When you take it out of the refrigerator, it will be very hard. Leave it at room temperature for at least 20 minutes to soften it before trying to roll it out. Flour your rolling pin and work surface and firmly tap the dough ball with the rolling pin to soften it.

Test for doneness by piercing the potatoes with a sharp knife or skewer.

There are certain people you meet over the course of your life whom you will never forget, and the person who gave me this recipe is one of them. Her name was Stella Wilson and she was from South Africa. I met her when I lived in Los Angeles many years ago. She had this captivating way about her and was living in L.A. as if she were still in her homeland, with Isak Dinesen chronicling her story. When I first had this unforgettable pie at her house, it was served by one of the most beautiful African men I have ever seen, dressed in a startling white butler's jacket with a diagonal red ribbon, which was proper South African dress, right down to a pair of white gloves.

MAKES ONE 9-INCH PIE

For the crust

1 cup (2 sticks) butter, plus extra for greasing the pie pan
1 cup vegetable shortening
1 cup boiling water
2 cups all-purpose flour
pinch of salt

For the filling

6 potatoes, peeled and sliced ¼ inch thick (russets or Idaho potatoes are fine)
1 large onion, thinly sliced
2 tablespoons chopped fresh parsley leaves
2 tablespoons butter, cut into small pieces
1 large egg, beaten
¼ cup freshly grated Parmesan cheese
1½ cups heavy cream

1. Combine 1 cup of the butter and all the remaining ingredients for the crust together in a medium-size bowl and mix well. The butter and shortening will melt and the mixture will be soupy. It will firm up after chilling. Press the dough into a ball and wrap in plastic. Chill overnight.

2. Preheat the oven to 350°F. Cut the dough into two even-size balls. Roll out one ball on a lightly floured work surface to about ¼ inch thick. Place the

rolled-out circle in a buttered, deep 9-inch pie plate. Layer the sliced potatoes, onion, and parsley in the dish and dot the final layer with the pieces of butter. Roll out the second dough ball to the same thickness and place it over the filling. Crimp the edges of the top and bottom crusts together with a fork and trim around the edge. Make eight to ten 1-inch slits all around the top of the crust. Brush the top crust with the beaten egg and sprinkle generously with the Parmesan cheese.

3. Bake for 20 minutes and then pour 4 to 6 tablespoons of the cream, little by little, through the slits. Repeat with more cream every 20 to 30 minutes until the cream is gone. Bake until the crust is golden brown and the potatoes are tender, about 1½ hours. Serve hot.

ENDIVE AND
MANDARIN ORANGE SALAD

ELLEN'S TIPS

Don't refrigerate the greens for more than 2 hours once they've been washed and trimmed.

If you like, you can use chives or red onion slices instead of the scallions.

You can also add some drained and rinsed cannellini beans or gar-banzo beans, or canned beets, for an even more interesting combination.

When you are serving steak along with potatoes as rich as Potato Pie South African Style is, it's always a good idea to have something crisp and clean and crunchy as a change of pace, especially before you serve a sweet baked dessert, like the brownies in this menu. The mandarin oranges add just the right delicate touch of sweetness here.

For the salad

2 Belgian endive, washed, patted dry, and split lengthwise
2 small bunches arugula, washed, patted dry, and stems trimmed
½ medium-size cucumber, peeled and sliced
2 scallions (white and light green parts), trimmed and chopped
Mandarin orange slices (canned is best)

For the dressing

½ cup olive oil
2 tablespoons freshly squeezed lemon juice
1 tablespoon soy sauce
¼ teaspoon freshly ground white pepper
1 teaspoon sesame oil

1. Place the greens in the salad bowl, then add the cucumber. Garnish with the scallions, cover with a clean kitchen towel, and refrigerate until ready to serve.

2. Combine the dressing ingredients until well mixed. Pour over the salad and toss to coat evenly. Garnish with the Mandarin oranges and serve.

AUNT SADYE'S
BROWNIES

Faye, Heni, Sadye, Kathy, and Anna were five sisters from Nebraska who moved to Los Angeles, and I met them because Heni was my friend Soni's mother. It sort of sounds like a Broadway musical. Why any of this matters is because Sadye was the best cook of the five sisters. Her brownies were and still are unforgettable. Thus are good recipes passed along. If ever anyone deserved brownies, even à la mode with Homemade Vanilla Ice Cream (page 26), runners do after running in the 10K race.

MAKES 24 SQUARES

> *1 cup (2 sticks) unsalted butter, plus extra for the baking dish*
> *1 cup all-purpose flour, plus extra for the baking dish*
> *4 ounces unsweetened chocolate*
> *4 large eggs*
> *2 cups sugar*
> *1 tablespoon pure vanilla extract*
> *pinch of salt*
> *1/2 cup walnut halves (optional), broken into pieces*

1. Preheat the oven to 350°F.

2. Grease and flour the bottom of an 8-inch square glass baking dish. Tap out any excess flour.

3. Melt 1 cup of the butter and chocolate together in a large pot set over medium-high heat or in a microwave. Allow to cool, then add the eggs, one at a time, mixing with a wooden spoon after each one. Add the sugar, flour, vanilla, salt, and walnuts, if desired. Do not overmix; fifty strokes ought to do it.

4. Pour the batter evenly into the prepared dish. Bake until a toothpick inserted in the center is still a little wet if you like a fudgy brownie, cleaner if you like a cakelike brownie, 40 to 45 minutes. Let cool a bit before cutting into squares.

ELLEN'S TIPS

Do not mix the batter with an electric mixer. Mix only by hand.

The good thing about a microwave is its ability to melt butter and chocolate in a glass measuring cup or microwave-safe ceramic bowl. It takes about 40 seconds.

The preparation only takes 5 minutes to do in one pot or bowl. That's the beauty of this recipe.

SUMMER

SUMMER

My first memories of Bridgehampton are shared with so many other people I know—they are of summer weekends, unforgettable summer weekends. We first started going out there in 1971. At the time, I had three small children and we were living in an apartment in New York City. Summer arrived that year, and it became clear that all of us needed a place to go. Good friends of ours suggested Bridgehampton as a place we might like to try. It seemed like a good idea.

We drove out one weekend and I have never forgotten my first impressions. Bridgehampton had huge, flat flowering potato fields on either side of the two-lane road into the village; lovely old trees that lined the main road; and sleepy one-story white wooden buildings in the village itself. We drove down to the beach, where the sand met the sky and the ocean stretched as far as you could see. The openness and feeling of space was what got me. We didn't need any convincing; this was the place for us. We rented a house for the month of August that summer—and for years after that. That first house was a small cottage—actually, it was more like a shack very close to those potato fields—where we had some of the happiest summers of our lives.

Nothing stays the same, as much as you'd like it to, and it was inevitable that Bridgehampton and all the other Hamptons, for that matter, would become more and more popular, which is exactly what has happened over the years. The last weekend in May is when "the season" starts. Early on Friday afternoons, the steady stream of cars arrives, inching its way down Route 27 and down Main Street, heading east. On Sunday nights, the stream reverses itself, like a long line of ants, making its way home. On summer weekends, you can set your watch by the amount of traffic. It's like a tide coming in and going out every weekend, rain or shine. We've learned to do our shopping early on Fridays—or better yet on Thursdays.

And yes, while there are undoubtedly more cars and crowds and congestion in Bridgehampton during the summer in particular, why people want to put up with it all makes perfect sense. There are probably more reasons to visit than ever before. At one time it was a quiet summer resort. Now it's a lifestyle, a sophisticated summer destination. There are tons of things to do—from simple picnic lunches at the best beaches in the world to the fanciest events and benefits. But Bridgehampton is still lovely and charming and even captivating in its own way. For some, it is all the social life; for us, it is a piece of land on the north side of the highway that offers privacy and pleasure.

Our house is our haven, no doubt about it, and during the summer it is busy with family and friends. My daughters, their husbands, and their children all come to stay for part or all of August. With any luck, we see my son, David, who grew up around here and has lots of friends to spend time with. Even Joe's daughter, Tiffany, who lives in Houston, makes a visit. Joe takes as many three-day weekends as he can over the summer and at least one weeklong vacation when time allows. A weekend doesn't go by when we don't have friends for supper either Friday or Saturday night or for Sunday lunch. It sounds like a lot to be doing, but I make sure that it isn't. I've gotten past that problem of entertaining, where for days in advance of company coming for dinner, I'd be squirreled away in the kitchen. I finally realized that I no longer needed to prove anything to anybody. I have come to accept the fact that simple is best. It works because it is real and can still be elegant. And, the foods of summer, especially, are so easy to prepare and enjoy.

Most lunches and dinners we have are on the terrace just off the kitchen. The view straight out is of our neighboring horses and our garden. We planned the garden so that it blooms at different times, starting with spring peonies and iris and ending with an aggressive catmint that has a bluish purple flower and an aroma of mint at certain times of the day. Around the corner from the terrace is our vegetable and cutting garden, where early in the day I pick some dahlias that we grow year after year. There is no better flower for the bedrooms and the table. They are my absolute favorite. Almost always there is a wonderful breeze that starts at the ocean, about three miles out to the south, and finds its way straight to our house. The temperature may be high, but the air is never still.

My favorite haunts for the best produce of summer are our own garden, for home-grown tomatoes and radishes the size of golf balls, and Country Garden and Halsey Vegetable stand, which are my local farm stands and are both very close to our house. I also have my herb garden, a large pot outside the kitchen door, which I use all summer. The peach orchard stand, which only gets going when the peaches are ready for selling, sometime in mid-July, is another good place to go. Easily one of the highlights of any of our summer weekends is the abundance of good corn, tomatoes, peaches, et al. Fresh fish and good meat provide everything I could need for barbecues or picnics outside on a blanket in the shade of one of our lovely trees. We might take a late afternoon trip to Gibson's Beach, then back home for a dinner of Moroccan-Style Shish Kebabs (page 267) with friends. We might also be celebrating a holiday weekend, like Fourth of July, with fireworks exploding somewhere off in the distance. Whatever the

occasion, I plan the menu early and do whatever I can in advance, which means that I always have time for golf or tennis or sitting around the pool watching the children swim. It's meant to be relaxed and easy, and it's choreographed to be that way. I want as little as possible to do at the end when everyone has gathered. Lots of last-minute work is not my favorite thing.

We came to Bridgehampton those many years ago to get away from the city, the stress, and the crowds, and, in fact, it is Bridgehampton that has provided so much pleasure for all of us. Bridgehampton has changed in many ways and probably seems too busy in summer, but what made us want to come here remains the same. The summer days languish as the sun shines down effortlessly. The sky is open and wide and the nights are filled with stars. The picket fences all around are covered in climbing roses and the shingles on the houses get more weathered and more handsome every year. Even when it rains, Bridgehampton is a special place.

A summer weekend in Bridgehampton can be whatever you want it to be, as quiet or as crazy as you wish. If you're like us and want a taste of both, my advice is to make it easy, whatever it is. The menus that follow, each of which celebrates the best of summer in some way, are all simple yet delicious.

Dinner on the Summer Solstice

Serves 6

If I had my way, all dinners would be served early and end early. I love company and I love to cook, but Joe and I also love our solitude. When is the right moment to come and go, especially on the longest day of the year? There is still light close to nine o'clock on that evening in late June, and typically at that hour we are seated at the table on the terrace, having a great summer supper and probably just finishing dessert. The first course is a wonderful tomato soup that I have been making for years. I follow the soup with swordfish, bought that morning from the Seafood Shop in Wainscott, the next little town down from Bridgehampton. Sometime in the early afternoon I marinate it in a mixture of Chinese ingredients. It needs no more than 3 to 4 hours to become really flavorful. Then it is just a matter of turning on the grill. A simple terrific cucumber salad, one of the few recipes I have inherited from my mother, complements the fish. A fruit pie, simple as can be, no pastry to deal with, closes the meal.

Whether we are eating dinner with our children and their children or with old friends, simplicity is key for a meal like this. I use pink oval straw mats on the table. I mix and marry glasses, colorful napkins, and other accessories, making sure that it all works together and harmonizes. I like to serve the swordfish on the teal-and-black fish platter my daughter Lexie made for me when she was ten years old, or on individual plates, with the cucumber salad in one of my eBay transferware bowls. eBay has also been the source for old jelly glasses to serve wine in. They remind me of France, where they use little bistro glasses for wine. Finally, I serve this with a cold Italian Orvieto or Soave.

TOMATO CARROT SOUP

ELLEN'S TIPS

Make this soup ahead of time when you have extra time, and freeze it. It keeps for up to 2 months very well.

Wash all the sand from the leeks by immersing them in deep, cold water after you have split them lengthwise.

Sometimes I use 5 large cubes of chicken bouillon diluted in 5 cups of hot water in place of canned chicken broth.

This may be the best tomato soup I've ever tasted. It is obviously because of the way the tomatoes and carrots harmonize. The soup can be served hot or cold, in simple white bowls or large wine goblets. I sometimes use demitasse cups and serve the soup as a passed hors d'oeuvre. Then we don't need spoons. (It is lovely to sip soup and munch on little goodies during cocktail hour.) Be sure, though, to serve the soup with White House Saltines (page 215), a recipe I first tasted at the White House, which I requested and received from the U.S. Navy, which heads up the staff in the dining room, lovingly referred to as "the mess." Together they make the perfect first course.

2 leeks, white part only, washed well and chopped
¼ pound (6 medium-size) carrots, sliced
3 tablespoons butter
2 pounds ripe plum tomatoes or one 28-ounce can crushed tomatoes
1½ cups tomato juice
5 cups chicken broth (canned is fine)
1½ tablespoons tomato paste
½ teaspoon dried thyme
1 tablespoon firmly packed brown sugar (light or dark)
1 dried hot red pepper or ½ teaspoon red pepper flakes
2 tablespoons peeled and grated fresh ginger
4 cloves garlic, crushed
2 tablespoons fresh cilantro leaves, chopped, for garnish

In a large saucepan, cook the leeks, carrots, and butter over medium heat, about 5 minutes, stirring from time to time, until they are softened. Stir in the tomatoes, tomato juice, chicken broth, tomato paste, thyme, brown sugar, red pepper, ginger, and garlic and bring the liquid to a boil. Cover and simmer for 40 minutes. Discard the whole red pepper. Cool the soup, put it in batches in a food processor or blender, and process until smooth. Garnish with 1 teaspoon of chopped cilantro per serving.

TOMATO CARROT SOUP
WITH WHITE HOUSE SALTINES

WHITE HOUSE
SALTINES

My husband, Joe, worked at the White House during the Reagan years, and we frequently ate at the White House Mess, a dining room for staff, where they served these delicious little crackers. They shared this recipe with me, and I simply must share it with you. The crackers are easy to make, crisp and delicate. They disappear almost as fast as you can make them. I love them warm with soup or salad. They're even good with cheese.

12 saltine crackers
ice water
¼ cup (½ stick) butter, melted,
*   plus extra for the cookie sheet*

1. Preheat the oven to 400°F.

2. Float the saltines one at a time in ice water until well soaked, but not falling apart. Shake off the excess water from each cracker and place them carefully on a buttered cookie sheet. Use a soft pastry brush to coat the tops of the crackers with the melted butter.

3. Bake for 15 minutes, reduce the heat to 300°F, and continue baking until a nutty brown, about 45 minutes. When completely cooled, store in an airtight container for at least a week.

ELLEN'S TIP

After you reduce the heat, be careful to watch the crackers because they can turn from charming brown to unattractive black very quickly.

SWORDFISH MY WAY

ELLEN'S TIPS

There is no substitute for fresh fish. Wash it, pat it dry, and rub it with lemon, but most important, keep it cold before you cook it. If fish smells fishy, it's not fresh.

If you marinate the fish at room temperature it absorbs the flavor better. It shouldn't be left at room temperature for more than 1 hour.

I use this marinade for poultry and meats as well.

I like swordfish best when it has been grilled, but you can also bake or broil these steaks. And if you find yourself caught short for marinating time, simply put the marinade together, add the fish, cover, and let it sit for as long as possible (see Ellen's Tips). You'd be surprised at how much flavor this marinade imparts. With beautiful fish steaks, like swordfish, be careful not to overcook them.

> *six 1-inch-thick swordfish steaks*
> *(about ½ to ¾ pound each)*
> *¼ cup soy sauce*
> *2 tablespoons sesame oil*
> *1 tablespoon freshly squeezed lemon juice*
> *¼ cup sesame seeds*
> *3 cloves garlic, crushed and chopped*
> *one 2-inch piece fresh ginger, peeled and grated*
> *1 large onion, thinly sliced*
> *2 lemons, sliced into wedges*
> *3 tablespoons chopped fresh cilantro leaves,*
> *scallion greens, or chives, for garnish*

1. Wash and pat dry the swordfish steaks.

2. In a glass baking dish large enough to hold the steaks in a single layer, whisk together the soy sauce, sesame oil, and lemon juice, then stir in the sesame seeds, garlic, ginger, and onion. Place the steaks in the marinade, turning to coat them on both sides. Cover with plastic wrap and let marinate in the refrigerator for at least 1 hour or overnight.

3. Preheat the broiler. Transfer the fish to a shallow pan and broil the steaks 5 minutes per side, until the fish breaks away when you put in a fork and twist it. Be careful not to overcook it. Serve with a wedge of lemon and garnish with the cilantro.

SWORDFISH MY WAY

MOM'S MARINATED CUCUMBERS

ELLEN'S TIPS

Be sure to remove all the dill stems before chopping. The dill leaves should be very finely chopped.

Concerning dill: More is not better; less is best. It is a very strong herb.

This Mom is my mom, who taught me this recipe. It is an old recipe that she learned from her mother. My father adored these thinly sliced cucumbers, with their sweet-and-sour flavor, and I do, too. They are particularly good with swordfish; I like to serve them very cold. They would be equally delicious with salmon steaks. Make them the day before so that they can stand overnight in the refrigerator and absorb the dill flavor. The colder they are, the better.

> *3 large cucumbers, peeled and sliced very thinly*
> *2 teaspoons kosher salt*
> *⅔ cup cider vinegar*
> *3 teaspoons sugar*
> *3 tablespoons finely chopped fresh dill*
> *   or 2 teaspoons dried dill*

1. Put the cucumbers in a strainer, sprinkle the salt evenly over the slices, and set the strainer in a bowl or in the sink to catch the water. Cover the cucumbers with a sheet of plastic wrap and weigh them down with a can of unopened tomatoes or some other heavy object. The slices will wilt and soften. Let drain at room temperature or refrigerate 4 to 5 hours or overnight.

2. Pour off the drained liquid from the bowl. Rinse the salt off the cucumbers with cold running water, pat dry, and place in a serving bowl. In another small bowl, whisk together the vinegar and sugar until the sugar dissolves. Pour the mixture over the cucumbers, and add the dill. Toss the cucumbers well and let them marinate for 3 to 4 hours or overnight in the refrigerator.

CHICAGO CORN PUDDING

My friend Soni Karp (wife of the best margarita maker in the world, Bob Karp—see A Mexican Buffet After Tennis on page 221) shared this recipe with me when we were both pregnant with our first children. We were living near each other in San Francisco and learning how to cook. Soni now lives in Chicago, where she serves this pudding along with all kinds of meat dishes, to very happy guests. What's so good about it is that it is crunchy on top and creamy inside and gets a big boost of flavor from the green chiles.

two 10-ounce packages frozen corn kernels,
slightly defrosted (see Ellen's Tips)
or 7 ears of leftover fresh corn, kernels cut off

³⁄₄ cup (1¹⁄₂ sticks) butter, melted
3 large eggs
1¹⁄₂ cups sour cream
³⁄₄ cup yellow cornmeal
1¹⁄₂ cups grated Monterey Jack cheese
one 4-ounce can green chiles, drained, patted dry,
and cut into ¹⁄₂-inch-wide strips
2 cloves garlic, crushed and chopped
salt and freshly ground black pepper to taste

1. Preheat the oven to 375°F.

2. Puree one package of the corn (or half of the fresh corn) in a food processor with all but 1 tablespoon of the melted butter and transfer to a large bowl. Add the eggs and sour cream and combine well. Fold in the other half of the corn. Set aside.

3. In a medium-size bowl, combine the cornmeal, grated cheese, chiles, and garlic and season with salt and pepper. Combine this with the corn mixture and mix well.

4. Use the remaining 1 tablespoon butter to grease a 2- or 3-quart casserole and pour in the corn batter. Bake until puffy and brown, about 1 hour. Serve immediately.

ELLEN'S TIPS

You don't need to use fresh corn in this recipe. If you have it around, that's great, but it makes very little difference. I only include the option.

Slightly defrost and separate the corn kernels so that they don't form an ice block in the food processor.

COLD BERRY PIE

ELLEN'S TIP

Never wash raspberries, blackberries, or boysenberries. They are too soft and absorbent and will become mushy. Strawberries and blueberries may be washed. Strawberries must be washed because of their pitted surface.

This is not a pie exactly. It has three different kinds of berries and it requires no cooking at all. Sound like the ideal summer dessert? You are right, and it deserves a high place on your summer dessert list. Find fresh berries, layer them with sour cream and brown sugar, and chill overnight. Then serve on the summer solstice—or anytime during the summer—in pretty glass bowls.

MAKES ONE 9-INCH PIE

1 pint fresh blackberries, picked over (see Ellen's Tips)
1 pint fresh raspberries, picked over (see Ellen's Tips)
1 pint fresh blueberries, picked over and washed
one 16-ounce container sour cream
1½ cups firmly packed brown sugar (light or dark)

Mix the berries gently together in a large bowl. Layer the bottom of a 9-inch pie dish with one third of the berries, then spread over a third of the sour cream, and sprinkle evenly with a third of the brown sugar. Repeat the layering two more times. Refrigerate for at least 2 hours, then cut like a pie in wedges.

A Mexican Buffet
After Tennis

BOB'S MARGARITAS

GUACAMOLE

TORTILLA SOUP

CHICKEN ENCHILADAS VERDES

BIG GREEN SALAD

MEXICAN FLAN WITH RASPBERRIES

Serves 6 to 8

The best time to play tennis in the summer in Bridgehampton is in the morning, while it is still cool. My husband is a fierce competitor who likes to challenge anyone who is willing. When he was working at the White House, he used to play a weekly Saturday doubles game with then–Vice President George Bush. I would sit in the "cheering section" with Barbara Bush, sipping iced tea and talking about everything from the press to face-lifts.

Now he will play with various friends, anywhere there is a good game.

This is my favorite lunch to serve when he comes home because all of it can be made in advance (except for the margaritas). I am never quite sure how many people there will be so I plan to serve it as a buffet. I like to serve this food casually and offer a selection—in this case, tortilla soup, enchiladas, a big salad, and a silky smooth custard for dessert. Guests can have the

option of just how much they want to eat. Soup and salad is fine, and so is a taste of everything, from soup to flan.

I like to serve the buffet outside on the terrace, under the pergola, which is covered with wisteria and clematis, providing welcome shade. I use a green gingham tablecloth and different-colored bandanas for napkins for fun. (Buy them at the Army-Navy surplus store.) I wrap the silverware in the bandanas and place the bundles in a big basket. Along the length of the table, down the center, I place small bowls for all the condiments that accompany the soup—chopped avocado, chopped onion, minced cilantro leaves, and grated Monterey Jack cheese. The bowls, plus the colors of the accompaniments themselves, are the centerpiece. I make sure to have a bottle of hot sauce for those who like it *picante*. Sometimes I decorate the table with little cactus plants.

The enchiladas come straight from the oven, hot and bubbling. If the day is very warm, I keep the flan in the refrigerator until the last possible minute. Its cool silkiness is a great antidote to a spicy Mexican meal and a long game of tennis on a summer day. All that remains is to enlist a good margarita maker to whip up the drinks.

BOB'S MARGARITAS

ELLEN'S TIP

I suggest you prepare your frozen salted glasses in advance so you can whip up these margaritas whenever.

I used to think that margaritas were hard to make and that the only way to have a really good one was out at a Mexican restaurant. Wrong. Bob Karp, husband of Soni, whose recipe for Chicago Corn Pudding (page 219) I've relied on since I can remember, is a longtime friend and a well-known, highly respected heart surgeon. He's also a decent tennis player, a wine connoisseur, and an even better margarita-maker. One time, while visiting in Michigan, he went to seven stores to find limeade, which took 2 hours. He was not happy but gave himself one extra margarita as compensation. I haven't developed his finesse in the mixing department, but I do know this: Really good margaritas, like these, are made one batch at a time.

> *1 cup cracked ice (8 ounces)*
> *one 8-ounce can frozen limeade concentrate*
> *8 ounces tequila (silver or gold)*
> *2 ounces triple sec*
> *3 to 4 tablespoons margarita salt*
> *one 3-inch piece lemon peel*

1. Put the ice in a blender, add the frozen limeade, tequila, and triple sec, and blend until the ice is chopped up.

2. Lay out a sheet of wax paper and put the salt on it. Rub the outside edge of each margarita glass with the lemon peel. The lemon oil provides enough moisture to make the salt stick. Press the edge of each glass into the salt and freeze them until you are ready to use. They will keep in the freezer for several days.

Opposite: **BOB'S MARGARITAS**

3. Pour the drink into the prepared glass and enjoy.

GUACAMOLE

I just don't believe it matters which avocados you buy, as long as they are ripe. I buy Hass avocados or the smooth-skinned variety (usually three or four at a time) and let them get soft to the touch. (Put them next to some bananas to ripen them quickly.) I think it is the red onion that puts this guacamole over the top.

>*2 ripe avocados, peeled and pitted (keep one of the pits)*
>*1 medium-size ripe tomato, chopped*
>*1 small red onion, chopped*
>*juice of 1 lemon*
>*salt and freshly ground black pepper to taste*
>*dash of Tabasco sauce*

In a medium-size bowl, mash the avocados. Add the tomato and onion to the mashed avocados and mix with a fork. Add the lemon juice and season with salt, pepper, and Tabasco. Push the reserved pit into the mixture to keep it from turning brown. Cover with plastic wrap and refrigerate until ready to serve. Serve with taco chips.

ELLEN'S TIPS

You can store guacamole in the refrigerator for one day if you keep the pit pressed into the mixture and wrap the guacamole well.

You can also serve guacamole with toasted bagel chips or on endive leaves as a predinner munchie.

TORTILLA SOUP

If you're a fan of tortilla soup, which I am, you will love this recipe. I have experimented with different types of tortilla soups, some spicy, some not so spicy, some thick, some not so thick, some with a few vegetables, some with too many vegetables—and this one is my favorite.

Do the lion's share of the preparation ahead of time. Poach the chicken and shred it and bake the tortillas strips. Be sure to pick out rustic bowls to serve all the garnishes in. That adds to the look.

ELLEN'S TIP

Add more tomato juice from the canned tomatoes if you need to thin the soup.

For the condiments

1 whole chicken breast (about 1 pound)
1 cup chicken broth (canned is fine)
1 cup grated Monterey Jack cheese
*1 ripe avocado, peeled, pitted, and cut into
    1-inch pieces, sprinkled with lemon juice*

For the soup

ten 6-inch corn tortillas
vegetable oil spray
½ cup olive oil
6 to 8 cloves garlic, to your taste, finely chopped
2 cups finely chopped onions
1½ teaspoons ground cumin
1 teaspoon ground coriander
½ teaspoon cayenne pepper
1 teaspoon salt
one 28-ounce can coarsely chopped tomatoes, drained
7 cups chicken broth (canned is fine)

1. Place the chicken breast in a medium-size saucepan with the chicken broth, cover, and bring to a low simmer. Cook over medium heat until just cooked through, 10 to 12 minutes. Drain the chicken and let cool. Remove the skin and bones and discard. Shred the chicken into bite-size pieces.

2. Preheat the oven to 350°F.

continued

3. To make the soup, take the tortillas and cut them into ½-inch-wide strips. Put the strips on a baking sheet, spray with the vegetable oil, and bake until crispy and golden, 12 to 15 minutes, depending on your oven. Remove from the oven and set aside.

4. In a medium-size saucepan, heat the olive oil over medium heat, then brown the garlic, stirring. Add the onions, cumin, coriander, and cayenne and stir until soft. Add the salt, tomatoes, and one third of the crispy tortilla strips. Add the chicken broth and cook for about 15 minutes more. Let cool, then puree the soup in batches in a blender.

5. Serve hot with the remaining crispy tortilla strips, the cheese, avocado, and chicken in small bowls for people to help themselves.

TORTILLA SOUP

CHICKEN ENCHILADAS VERDES

ELLEN'S TIPS

Tomatillos and long green chile peppers can be purchased at any good gourmet grocery store.

The green tomatillo sauce can be made ahead and frozen. Defrost and reheat to use.

You will note that I suggest that you poach the chicken breasts in chicken broth instead of plain water. It is a way to keep flavor in the meat.

Cilantro acts as a sweetener and can balance a sauce that's too hot.

If you find that the chile peppers are large, you might want to use only one. Be sure to taste them.

Picture this: chicken with a dollop of creamy cheese all wrapped up in a soft tortilla baked and topped with a lemony, light green sauce made from fresh tomatillos. What is there not to like? Well, plenty, if the balance is off. We've all had our share of really heavy enchiladas verdes. These enchiladas are at the absolute opposite end of the spectrum. They are rich and creamy but have a light lovely flavor. They are also easy to make.

For the cream cheese filling

two 3-ounce packages cream cheese, softened
¹/₂ cup heavy cream
3 whole chicken breasts (about 3 pounds), split into 6 halves
1 cup chicken broth (canned is fine)

For the sauce

2 long green chile peppers (see Ellen's Tips)
10 tomatillos, husked and stemmed
2 teaspoons chopped fresh cilantro leaves
³/₄ cup chicken broth (canned is fine)
1 teaspoon salt
¹/₂ teaspoon freshly ground white pepper
1¹/₂ cups heavy cream
1 large egg

To finish the enchiladas

2 tablespoons vegetable oil
ten to twelve 8-inch flour tortillas
³/₄ cup chopped onion
1 cup grated Monterey Jack cheese

1. To make the filling, mash the cream cheese and heavy cream together in a medium-size bowl and set aside.

2. Place the chicken breasts with the chicken broth in a large skillet over medium-high heat and poach the chicken, covered, until cooked through, about 20 minutes or so. Remove the skin and bones and discard. Shred the chicken into bite-size pieces and set aside.

3. To make the sauce, place the chile peppers, tomatillos, cilantro, chicken broth, salt, pepper, heavy cream, and egg in a food processor and process until smooth.

4. Preheat the oven to 350°F.

5. To finish the enchiladas, heat the oil in a large skillet over medium heat. Cook the tortillas 30 seconds on each side in the hot oil and drain them on a paper towel.

6. Fill each tortilla with some shredded chicken and 1 tablespoon of the cream cheese mixture. Add 1 tablespoon of the chopped onion, roll up the tortillas, and place seam side down in a large glass baking dish. Pour the green sauce over, then top with the grated Monterey Jack cheese. Bake for 20 minutes, covered, then uncover for 10 minutes more to brown the top. Serve hot.

Big Green Salad with
Ellen's Dressing

You'll see throughout this book that I serve a lot of different kinds of salads—mixed greens, romaine, iceberg, watercress. For me, salad is an important part of a menu, especially when I am serving anything buffet style. For someone who makes as many salads as I do, it's necessary to have a really great dressing, and I do have two good ones. I leave it to you to decide which one you prefer. You can't go wrong with either, on any salad green.

> *1 head red lettuce, washed and dried*
> *1 head Boston lettuce, washed and dried*
> *1 Belgian endive, washed, cored, and split lengthwise*
> *12 to 16 cherry tomatoes, washed and halved*
> *½ cup dressing of your choice (recipes follow)*

1. Choose the very best and sweetest leaves from the lettuce. Trim the lettuce, then wash and pat or spin dry. Wrap the lettuce and endive loosely in paper towels until you use them or put them directly in your salad bowl and cover with a clean, dry dish towel. Refrigerate.

2. Add the cherry tomatoes just before serving. Toss well with the dressing and serve.

Ellen's Dressing, I and II

I've been making the first of these two salad dressings for about thirty five years. God only knows who gave it to me first, but it is easily the best dressing I've ever had. The proportions are standard three parts oil to one part vinegar, but the ingredients are what make it so good. I store it in a mayonnaise jar that I never refrigerate because it is best kept at room temperature. Trust me, if you eat salads 2 or 3 times a week or more, this dressing will be gone before it can go bad.

I concocted Version II maybe ten years ago, and I love it just as much as the original. Whichever one you make, remember to shake it well right before using it. You also know the rule: Less dressing is more. Never drench a salad. If there's even a little extra in the bottom of the salad bowl, the greens were over-dressed.

MAKES 1 CUP

Version I

¾ cup good-quality olive oil
¼ cup good-quality red wine vinegar
1 teaspoon Colman's dry mustard
1 teaspoon salt
1 teaspoon sugar
4 cloves garlic, crushed to a paste

Version II

¾ cup good-quality olive oil
1 tablespoon balsamic vinegar
1 tablespoon good-quality red wine vinegar
1 teaspoon sugar
2 cloves garlic, crushed to a paste

Put all the ingredients in a jar and shake well.

Mexican Flan
with Raspberries

ELLEN'S TIPS

When you mix the eggs and other ingredients make sure you do not use an electric mixer. You don't want any bubbles to form. Bubbles make air and air makes holes in the custard. Mix thoroughly but gently.

The flan usually doesn't come out of the mold the first time. But take care not to overdo the time on the next dipping. Be patient.

This recipe for flan actually comes straight from Mexico, via an adorable friend of my daughter Claudia, whose name is also Claudia, Claudia Nicolayevsky. Her parents came from Russia to Mexico City. Claudia, or Nick as she's called, passed this way of making flan along to me. Made with both condensed and evaporated milks, it is sweet and velvety. It can be served at room temperature or cold. For a summer lunch after tennis, I serve it very cold, with raspberries. It makes a good closing note to a Mexican feast.

> *½ cup sugar*
> *6 large eggs*
> *one 8-ounce can sweetened condensed milk*
> *one 8-ounce can evaporated milk*
> *1 tablespoon pure vanilla extract*

1. Preheat the oven to 350°F.

2. Melt the sugar in a small, heavy saucepan over low heat until it is light brown; do not stir it. Carefully pour the melted sugar into a mold (I use a 3-cup ring mold). Tilt the mold around so that the sugar coats the insides evenly. Set aside.

3. Using a wooden spoon, mix the eggs, condensed and evaporated milks, and vanilla together in a large bowl. Pour the mixture into the prepared mold. Place the mold in a larger pan filled with water to come halfway up the side of the mold. (This is called a water bath, or bain marie.)

4. Place in the center of the oven and bake until set, about 20 minutes. Remove from the water bath and allow to cool completely before unmolding.

5. To unmold, dip the ring in hot water for 10 seconds and invert onto a cold plate. If it doesn't come out the first time, dip it again for 5 seconds until it does. Refrigerate the flan.

Allie's Birthday Dinner

NEW YORK'S FINEST CHICKEN SALAD

STUFFED SHELLS WITH RED SAUCE

GARLIC BREAD

CAESAR SALAD

CHOCOLATE CLOUD CAKE WITH M&M'S

Serves 8

Birthdays are really happy occasions in our family, and usually we celebrate around a wonderful meal. Even the youngest family members, my adorable grandchildren—Allie, who is six, Jonathan, who is four, and Kelsey, almost two—get their pick of a specially cooked meal. July 2 is Allie's birthday and we love it when she can join us in Bridgehampton for a party just for her. We eat on the terrace with a table for Allie and a few of her little pals. One year I decorated the table with Barbie dolls. Jonathan likes a table of his own, with trucks as his centerpiece. The parents and grandparents gather at yet another table as we gaze at our progeny. We don't need anything but flowers on ours, and maybe one Barbie to remind us why we're all together!

We discovered very early on that Allie loves chocolate and the chocolate cake she likes best—Chocolate Cloud Cake—is absolutely ethereal. I write her name and age on the top with multicolored M&M's. That's a big hit. As for the rest of the menu, there is nothing complicated about any of it. The stuffed shells are pure comfort food and the cake is the perfect chocolate birthday cake. One thing I learned the hard way: Remember to have plenty of cold milk in the fridge. (It's the adults who want milk with the cake!) But if the adults would like a glass of wine with dinner, try serving a good Italian Valpolicella or Montepulciano.

NEW YORK'S FINEST
CHICKEN SALAD

I remember when I first started serving a tray of nibbles—predinner treats—on a Japanese tray, much like a bento box. It was a good plan. The look of the tray is quite stunning, with its black lacquer shine. All you need is a set of small bowls to hold the goodies.

For Allie's party, I keep the nibbles simple: olives, salted nuts (or Japanese-style soy mixed nuts and crackers), or popcorn. If I feel the need for more, I add a platter of endive spears stuffed with New York's Finest Chicken Salad. A friend of mine named Mike is a New York City police officer, and he taught me this recipe, ergo its name! Here it is.

> 1½ cups cooked white chicken meat,
>   very finely minced or ground up
> 2 tablespoons grated onion with its juices
> 3 tablespoons mayonnaise
> 3 tablespoons finely diced celery
> salt and freshly ground black pepper to taste
> 1 Belgian endive
> 1 tablespoon chopped fresh chives, for garnish

1. Put the chicken in a food processor and pulse to chop finely. Transfer to a medium-size bowl and add the grated onion. Fold in the mayonnaise and celery and mix with a fork to combine into a smooth paste. Season with salt and pepper and set aside.

2. Rinse the endive and core the center blossom from it. Separate the leaves and gently dry them with paper towels or spin-dry. Place 2 tablespoons of chicken salad on each leaf and garnish with the chopped chives. Serve on a pretty plate.

ELLEN'S TIP

You can serve this chicken salad as a dip along with crackers or bagel chips instead of the endive leaves.

STUFFED SHELLS WITH RED SAUCE

ELLEN'S TIP

Cherry peppers come in a glass jar in brine. Under cold water I rinse off the one I plan to use before dropping it into the sauce, being careful not to break it. After the pepper has cooked, I take it out, remove the stem, chop it finely, and put it in a small bowl for those who really want some extra spice. If you are making this dish for adults only, you can use two or three peppers.

You know you have a winner of a recipe when children devour it, and this one kids just love. It shouldn't be surprising: pasta shells with a creamy ricotta filling in a light tomato sauce. I add one cherry pepper to the sauce while it cooks. I picked this up years ago from my friend Ben Gazzara, who taught me a marvelous red sauce. This small pepper adds a hint of zest but doesn't make the sauce too hot.

For the red sauce

3 tablespoons olive oil
5 cloves garlic, crushed
two 28-ounce cans crushed tomatoes
1 teaspoon dried basil
1 teaspoon red wine vinegar or balsamic vinegar
1 cherry pepper (see Ellen's Tip)

For the shells

2 teaspoons olive oil
1 teaspoon salt
two 1-pound boxes jumbo pasta shells

For the filling

two 15-ounce containers ricotta cheese
4 large eggs
½ cup freshly grated Parmesan cheese, plus more for serving

butter for the baking dish
4 to 5 tablespoons chopped fresh parsley leaves

1. To make the sauce, heat the olive oil in a large skillet over medium heat. Add the garlic and cook, stirring, until lightly browned. Add the tomatoes, basil, vinegar, and pepper and simmer for 15 minutes. Transfer to a bowl and set aside.

continued

STUFFED SHELLS WITH RED SAUCE,
GARLIC BREAD, AND CAESAR SALAD

2. Preheat the oven to 350°F.

3. To make the shells, bring a large pot of water to a boil. Add the olive oil and salt, then add the shells. Bring back to a boil and let boil until the shells are *al dente* (still a little chewy). Drain and let cool enough to handle.

4. In a large bowl, combine the ricotta, eggs, and Parmesan with a fork until well mixed. Put 1 tablespoon of the stuffing in each shell with a small spoon and lay the shells side by side in a buttered 9 × 12-inch baking dish. At this point the shells can be covered tightly with plastic wrap and refrigerated overnight.

5. Pour the red sauce over the shells, just enough to cover and moisten them. Bake in the oven for 30 minutes. Sprinkle with the chopped parsley and serve with the extra sauce and a bowl of Parmesan cheese on the side.

GARLIC BREAD

There are two reasons for making your own garlic bread. The first is that it is ridiculously easy to do; the second is that when you're the cook, you get to determine just how much garlic to use. I like a lot of fresh garlic, but feel free to use less, if you want. Be sure to serve the loaf straight from the oven—hot garlic bread is in a class by itself. Nothing compares to the heavenly smell of garlic bread as it bakes. And if you're short on time, see my tip for Quick Garlic Bread.

> *1 cup (2 sticks) butter, softened*
> *¼ cup chopped fresh parsley leaves*
> *2 cloves garlic, very finely minced*
> *½ teaspoon salt*
> *¼ teaspoon freshly ground black pepper*
> *1 loaf Italian bread or French baguette*

1. Preheat the oven to 375°F.

2. In a medium-size bowl, combine the butter, parsley, garlic, salt, and pepper and mash well.

3. Cut the loaf of bread lengthwise and spread both halves with the butter mixture. Place the two halves together and wrap with aluminum foil.

4. Bake in the oven until the butter has melted, about 10 minutes. Unwrap and place the halves side by side on the foil and bake until the edges begin to brown, an additional 8 minutes. Let cool slightly, cut into pieces, and serve.

ELLEN'S TIPS

You can keep the bread wrapped in foil for up to 30 minutes, but after that it will dry out.

Another way to do this is to cut the bread in diagonal slices and spread each slice with plain softened butter and then sprinkle each slice with garlic salt or garlic powder. Wrap the loaf in foil and bake for 20 minutes in a 300°F oven. This is a faster way; the bread is soft and garlicked.

Make sure the garlic is very finely minced or it will taste bitter.

CAESAR SALAD

This is admittedly a very modified Caesar salad. There is no raw egg, only one anchovy fillet, and barely any garlic, except in the dressing. The grown-ups will like this dressing; as for my granddaughter Allie, when she was three or four she used to ask, "Is it 'picy, Nana?"

Fix this salad according to the company you are hosting. Use more anchovies, if you like. I cut off the very dark green of the bigger leaves and use the inner leaves of the romaine head. They are extra sweet and crunchy and very pretty. You will need at least two heads of romaine for eight servings.

> *2 heads romaine lettuce*
> *1 anchovy fillet*
> *⅔ cup Ellen's Dressing (page 232)*
> *1 cup freshly grated Parmesan cheese*

1. Clean and separate the romaine lettuce, discarding the tough outside leaves. Spin the leaves to dry completely, or pat dry with paper towels. Set aside in the refrigerator wrapped loosely in a clean dish towel.

2. Mash the anchovy fillet with a fork and mix into the salad dressing.

3. When ready to serve, toss the lettuce with the dressing and Parmesan, reserving 1 tablespoon of the cheese to sprinkle on at serving time. With a slotted spoon, place several leaves on a salad plate for each guest, sprinkle on the cheese, and serve immediately.

CHOCOLATE CLOUD CAKE
WITH M&M'S

I have Theresa, who lives in Washington, D.C., and is a friend of my daughter, Claudia, to thank for this fabulous recipe. Theresa discovered it during her years growing up in the Deep South. The cake is dense but also light and wonderfully moist on account of the buttermilk and self-rising flour. It is indeed an unusual cake.

The first time Allie tasted chocolate cake she was age one, and with each bite she clapped her hands. It was adorable, so I decorate with multicolored M&M's on top and around the edge of the cake as the border. Would Allie say this is the best chocolate cake ever? Yes, at the ripe old age of six she would. I couldn't agree more.

For the cake

vegetable shortening for greasing the pan
2½ cups sifted self-rising flour, plus
    2 tablespoons for the pan
    (see Ellen's Tips)
1 cup (2 sticks) margarine, softened
2 cups sugar
2 large eggs
¾ cup unsweetened cocoa powder
    (Hershey's is fine)
1 teaspoon pure vanilla extract
1 cup buttermilk (see Ellen's Tips)
½ teaspoon baking soda
1 cup boiling water

For the icing

½ cup (1 stick) butter, softened
6 tablespoons milk
3 tablespoons unsweetened cocoa powder
    (Hershey's is fine)
one 16-ounce box confectioners' sugar
1 teaspoon pure vanilla extract
½ cup chopped pecans (optional)

continued

ELLEN'S TIPS

You must use self-rising flour. It makes a big difference because it produces a full, silky, soft cake.

If you don't have buttermilk, you can make it by combining 1 cup milk with 2 teaspoons white vinegar in a sealed jar and letting it ferment for 30 minutes or so at room temperature. It will clot up a bit and, voilà, you have buttermilk.

This recipe can be doubled to make a larger sheet cake, measuring 16 × 20 inches.

Do not substitute butter for margarine here. It ruins the cake.

If decorating with M&M's, leave the chopped pecans out.

CHOCOLATE CLOUD CAKE WITH M&M'S

1. Preheat the oven to 350°F. Grease the sides and bottom of a Pyrex sheet pan, approximately 8 × 13 inches, with shortening. Flour the pan with 2 tablespoons flour and tap out any excess and set aside.

2. Cream the margarine and sugar together in a large bowl. Add eggs one at a time and mix well. Add the cocoa and vanilla and mix well. Combine the buttermilk and baking soda in a small bowl and add to the creamed mixture, alternating with the 2½ cups flour. Pour in the boiling water and mix slowly until well combined.

3. Pour the batter into the prepared pan and bake until a toothpick inserted in the center of the cake comes out clean, 30 to 35 minutes. Remove from the oven and let cool completely in the pan.

4. To make the icing, in a medium-size heavy saucepan, bring the butter, milk, and cocoa to a boil. Remove from the heat. Add the confectioners' sugar, vanilla, and pecans, if using, and mix well. Pour over the cake while the icing is still warm.

July Fourth Party
in the Garden

SAVORY TOASTS

POACHED SALMON WITH DILL SAUCE

CORN ON THE COB, THE WRIGHT WAY

STEAMED SPINACH

ROSE'S BLUEBERRY PIE

Serves 6 to 8

This holiday is a favorite in our house because of the fireworks. We always do a dinner to celebrate. I shop in the morning at my favorite farm stand, the Country Garden, two seconds from home, on Scuttle Hole Road. It's a simple Quonset hut, with an old tractor out front. They have vegetables, herbs, fresh flowers—whatever is in season—all displayed in bushel baskets or pails. I pick up my blueberries for the pie. I make an extra trip in the afternoon for freshly picked corn.

The house will fill with the smell of cinnamon and pie. At some point, Joe will take Allie and Jonathan to pick up the salmon and stop for the corn. Jonathan likes to sit on the tractor and pretend he is a big guy. We'll eat early in the garden on the round picnic table, which I've covered with a red, white, and blue star quilt. After supper, we might go down to the beach to see the fireworks that are set off along the coast. The night will be filled with muffled far-off bangs and sparkly lights that we can actually see from our backyard. The whole day reminds us of just how much we love these days in the good ole U.S. of A. And I always pick up a bottle or two of Washington State Chardonnay.

SAVORY TOASTS

ELLEN'S TIPS

You can also serve either of these two mixtures in a small serving bowl with crackers or with toasted pita bread wedges.

All of the ingredients for both versions should be very finely chopped.

Jacques Pépin demonstrated this recipe on television one time in 1991 and I wrote down what I could make of it. I thought it sounded so good and indeed it was. I have changed it around to suit my own taste, but there are still two options here: one is sweet (on account of the figs); the other is herby. One is cooked and one is not, so try both ways. They are each wonderful on their own served with a drink.

Version I

1 cup finely chopped Greek olives, rinsed and pitted
1 ounce flat anchovies, drained, patted dry, and finely chopped
5 dried figs, soaked in hot water to cover till softened, drained, and finely chopped
5 tablespoons olive oil
12 thin slices French bread, lightly toasted
6 tablespoons finely chopped fresh cilantro leaves

In a food processor, place the olives, anchovies, figs, and olive oil and pulse to a medium-fine paste. Spread each slice of bread with 2 teaspoons of the mixture and arrange on a pretty plate, garnished with the cilantro.

Version II

1 tablespoon extra-virgin olive oil
3 tablespoons finely chopped shallots
3 tablespoons finely chopped garlic
1/3 cup finely chopped Greek olives, rinsed and pitted
1/4 cup finely chopped mushroom caps
3 tablespoons finely chopped fresh parsley leaves
1 teaspoon finely chopped fresh mint leaves
a squeeze of lemon
12 thin slices French bread, lightly toasted

In a medium-size skillet over medium heat, heat the oil, then cook the shallots and garlic, stirring until soft and golden brown, about 4 minutes. Reduce the heat to low, add the olives and mushrooms, and cook another 3 minutes, stirring until well mixed. Remove the mixture from the heat and place in a small bowl. Add the parsley, mint, and a tiny bit of lemon juice, and mix to combine. Spread each slice of bread with 2 teaspoons of the mixture and arrange on a pretty plate.

POACHED SALMON WITH DILL SAUCE

ELLEN'S TIPS

If you prefer to use a whole salmon, place the fish in aluminum foil, add your ingredients, and seal the foil at the edges tightly, making a package around the fish, allowing room for the steam to poach it. When it is done, after about 1 hour, slide the whole fish onto a serving platter, discarding the seasonings. Peel the skin off carefully to make it look good. Add some lemon slices and/or some cucumber slices and a little of the sauce from the pan to keep it moist. Discard the remaining cooking liquid. Serve at room temperature.

Decorate with seeded lemon halves.

This salmon is definitely poached, but not in the way you might think. You will not need a fancy French fish poacher here. There is no court bouillon for those who are classically trained cooks and know what that is. You can use salmon steaks or a whole salmon. This salmon poaches with peeled cucumbers in heavy cream in a regular baking dish. I've never seen another recipe like it, and I can't remember where I found it, but I've had it since I was twenty-four years old and I always am amazed at how really good it is. It is ideal for summer entertaining because it can be served cold or, better yet, at room temperature.

eight 1½-inch-thick salmon steaks or one 3-pound whole salmon (see Ellen's Tips)
pinch of salt
freshly ground black pepper to taste
pinch of dried thyme
¼ cup (½ stick) butter, softened
1 small onion, thinly sliced
8 black peppercorns
4 sprigs fresh parsley
2 bay leaves
2 cloves garlic, crushed
2 medium-size cucumbers, cut in half lengthwise and seeded
2 cups light cream
Dill Sauce (page 254)

1. Preheat the oven to 350°F.

2. Rub the salmon steaks with the salt, pepper, and thyme. (If you are using a whole salmon, see Ellen's Tips.) Butter a glass baking dish large enough to hold the salmon in a single layer and coat both sides of the fish with 2 tablespoons of the butter. Put the onion slices on top of the fish, then add the peppercorns, parsley, bay leaves, garlic, cucumbers, and cream. Cover the dish tightly with a sheet of aluminum foil. Bake until the fish pulls away from the bone and is pale pink and fork-tender, 30 to 40 minutes, depending on the size of the fish. When it is done, discard the cucumbers, parsley, bay leaves, peppercorns, and cream. Serve with the Dill Sauce.

POACHED SALMON WITH DILL SAUCE
AND CORN ON THE COB, THE WRIGHT WAY

DILL SAUCE

Salmon and dill are a match made in heaven. I pick my dill from the garden at the last minute, then snip it finely with kitchen scissors, which is really the easiest way to do it. The amount of lemon juice here can be adjusted. I like this sauce a little tangy and saucy, meaning easy to pour. If you want a thicker sauce, use a little less lemon juice. Don't eliminate it entirely, though; it adds necessary flavor.

MAKES 1 CUP

1 cup mayonnaise

3 tablespoons finely chopped fresh dill

2 tablespoons freshly squeezed lemon juice

Combine the mayonnaise with the dill and lemon juice and mix with a fork until smooth. Chill well.

CORN ON THE COB,
THE WRIGHT WAY

Oh, the number of ways I have cooked fresh corn! There had to be a perfect way to do it. I can safely say, from years of experience, that this one comes closest. It helps, of course, that I am able to buy just-picked ears from the local farm stand two seconds from home. I enlist the help of Joe and my grandchildren to shuck the corn in the garden. It is a good project for kids. The way to butter the corn is a family tradition, which I love almost as much as the corn itself. You need slices of sturdy white, French, or Italian bread—and a stick of cold butter. Cut the slices in quarters and put in a basket. Take a generous pat of butter, put it on a piece of bread, and use the bread like a sponge to butter the corn. What happens, of course, is that the butter melts into the bread at the same time, making it quite edible. I've never known anyone—and that's a lot of corn eaters since we've been going to Bridgehampton—to be able to resist eating several ears of Long Island corn so smartly served.

14 to 16 ears fresh corn, shucked
3 teaspoons dried thyme

Fill a big pot with cold water. Put in the ears of corn and the thyme. Over high heat, bring the corn to a boil and turn the heat off. Remove the ears and place them in a basket with a large pretty napkin or a country dish towel.

ELLEN'S TIP

Remember to buy freshly picked corn. The sugar in corn turns to starch after about 8 hours from the time it is picked, and when you cook starchy corn it diminishes the wonderful sweetness that we all want.

STEAMED SPINACH

Don't be alarmed by the amount of spinach you have to buy here. Spinach wilts down to nothing once it's cooked. We don't plant spinach in our garden, so I buy the packaged, prewashed variety of fresh bunches of spinach. If you grow your own or buy it from a farm stand, wash it—not just rinse it—carefully. Wash the prewashed variety for that matter, because it still needs it. Sand is not part of the recipe.

4 pounds fresh spinach
1 tablespoon olive oil
2 tablespoons butter

1. Wash the spinach. Trim the large tough stems off and set in a colander to dry.

2. Heat the oil in a large skillet over medium-high heat. Place the spinach in the skillet and cook, covered, until wilted, about 5 minutes, tossing so that all the spinach gets cooked. Transfer the spinach to a platter and place the butter, sliced in pats, on top while it is still hot.

ROSE'S BLUEBERRY PIE

ELLEN'S TIPS

If the dough is refrigerated overnight, take it out for half an hour to get softer. It will be easier to work with.

Put a cookie sheet under the pie plate while you are baking the pie to prevent a mess in the oven should the berry juices boil over.

If there are some pink blueberries in your box, they are still ripe and usable.

If the edges of the crust are browning too fast, cover them with a strip of aluminum foil crimped to fit.

I first tasted this pie when my daughter Alexis was a baby in 1967. Rose Delaney made it. She was an Irish woman and had that type of wisdom that only the Irish have. She was always giving me advice, whether it was about the baby or anything else that occurred to her. I didn't always take her advice but it turned out I should have. I took her advice on this pie, however. She informed me that it was the best blueberry pie ever, and Rose was right. (For me, it's even better when you top it with Homemade Vanilla Ice Cream, page 26.)

MAKES ONE 9-INCH PIE

For the crust

2 1/2 cups all-purpose flour
1/2 cup (1 stick) unsalted butter
1/2 cup vegetable shortening
pinch of salt
1/3 cup ice water

For the filling

1 cup firmly packed brown sugar (light or dark)
1 tablespoon freshly squeezed lemon juice
5 tablespoons cornstarch
2 pints fresh blueberries, washed and picked over
2 tablespoons butter

1. To make the crust, place the flour, butter, shortening, and salt in the bowl of a food processor and pulse until the mixture resembles fine meal. Add the ice water and pulse until the dough comes together in a ball. Turn onto a lightly floured work surface and knead the dough 4 or 5 times or until the dough comes together. Divide the dough into two balls. Cover with plastic wrap and refrigerate, if possible, at least 1 hour or overnight.

2. Preheat the oven to 400°F. Roll out one ball of dough on a lightly floured work surface into a 12-inch circle about 1/4 inch thick. Fit the dough into the bottom of a 9-inch pie plate.

3. Place the brown sugar, lemon juice, and cornstarch in a medium-size bowl and toss with the blueberries. Pour the blueberry mixture into the pie plate. Dot with the butter. Roll out the second round of dough and place over the filling.

Crimp the edges together, sealing the bottom and top crusts. Trim around the edges of the pie to neaten up the crust. Make three to four slits on top with a sharp knife for the steam to escape while baking.

4. Bake for 15 minutes, then reduce the oven temperature to 350°F and bake until the crust is brown and the blueberries are bubbling, another 40 to 45 minutes. Serve the pie warm.

ROSE'S BLUEBERRY PIE

First August Weekend
with the Family—
and It's Pouring

Toasted Pita Bread with Hummus

Sorrel Soup

Moroccan-Style Shish Kebabs

Couscous à la Ellen

Strawberry Shortcakes

Serves 8

Each year, the first weekend in August reminds us all over again of why we built our house in Bridgehampton. Two of my daughters and their families arrive to stay for a while: Claudia, her husband, Andrew, and their children, Allie and Jonathan, come up from Washington, D.C. Lexie, her husband, Bill, and daughter, Kelsey, drive down from Weston, Connecticut. The married children and grandchildren are the ones who come to stay. I am delighted by their visit, I can tell you.

There is that lovely moment, when everyone arrives, that the house starts to hum. Eventually, everything settles down and we fall into our little routines. If it rains, and in the Hamptons you never can be sure whether it will, we move in to our indoor activities. We have a shelf of games in the library and we drag them out to keep occupied.

Supper that first night is a favorite of everyone, even if we've been shut in all day. We might be lucky to get some sun in the afternoon, so we can have our drinks or dessert, at least, outside on the terrace. I plan an easy-to-make meal that can be prepared in advance. I've found that is the only way to make something simple: Plan it ahead of time. I divide and conquer and I am not a bit shy about assigning tasks. For this dinner, the kids love to spear the lamb onto the skewers for the shish kebabs. One of my daughters will toast pita bread. The hummus is store-bought—there's nothing wrong with that. I help it out a bit by garnishing heavily with chopped cilantro leaves. The soup and biscuits I've made in advance. Because the couscous is such a snap, it can wait until later to be cooked. Have a bottle of Spanish Rioja (I like Ribero del Quero) on hand. It's so much more fun if everyone helps out.

A POSTSCRIPT: This is a Moroccan-inspired menu and you may wonder how Strawberry Shortcakes (page 270) made it onto the list. It is a favorite dessert of mine and I like to mix it up.

SORREL SOUP

There is a fun story behind this recipe. One summer I was visiting the Brokaws on their ranch in Montana. Meredith Brokaw's garden was bursting with sorrel, a green that I never associated with Montana. There was so much of it we both decided to make soup. Meredith wanted to try out a recipe of hers and I thought I'd compete with one of my own that I had in mind. My version got the blue ribbon, in my opinion, largely because of its thick and smooth consistency. Don't ever underestimate the competitiveness of yours truly or the power of a potato.

Sorrel is available only for a short time in the summer. It is a tender leafy green, with a lovely lemony flavor. Keep your eye out for it in June and into July, and when you see it, buy it.

continued

Campbell's makes a garlic-flavored potato soup, which comes in a 16-ounce can, that is wonderful for this soup.

Sliced lemon is also a good garnish.

A tablespoon of cooked rice may be added to each bowl of soup to make it a more hearty course.

As with many soups, it is
nice to serve in demitasse
cups to sip as an
hors d'oeuvre. You will
need a small spoon only
if you've added rice.

Scallions can substitute
for the chives, the green
part only.

You can make strong
chicken broth by combin-
ing 3 tablespoons of pow-
dered chicken base or 3
large bouillon cubes with 2
cups of boiling water.

This soup can be frozen
and reheated. You will
need to blend it one more
time before serving.

5 cups fresh sorrel, washed well and stemmed
2 tablespoons water
two 8-ounce cans potato soup, canned or frozen,
    or 2 large Idaho potatoes, peeled and diced
3 cups strong chicken broth (see Ellen's Tips),
    plus 2 tablespoons more, if needed
1 ½ cups heavy cream
freshly ground white pepper to taste
2 tablespoons chopped fresh chives
    (see Ellen's Tips)

1. In a covered saucepan over medium-high heat, cook the sorrel in the water until it wilts. Drain the water off and add the potato soup (or diced potatoes), chicken broth, and cream. Cook over low heat for about 15 minutes until it thickens, stirring constantly. Season with white pepper and let cool.

2. Puree the mixture in a blender. If it is too thick, dilute the soup with a few more tablespoons of chicken broth. Ladle into serving bowls and garnish each bowl with a scant teaspoon of finely chopped chives.

SORREL SOUP

MOROCCAN-STYLE SHISH KEBABS AND COUSCOUS À LA ELLEN

MOROCCAN-STYLE
SHISH KEBABS

ELLEN'S TIP

Cherry peppers can be bought in any grocery store. They are in glass jars in brine. Simply wash them under cold water before using.

Everybody grills year-round now, thanks to the "on" button on the ubiquitous gas grill, but I still, and forever, will associate grilling with summer, when it is warm outside. Just as the light starts to fade, Joe starts up the grill for these shish kebabs, which are served with two sauces—one is plain cumin powder and the other is a *sofrito* (something fried up) that is quite spicy. Joe and my daughter Claudia like it hot; Lexie, Andrew, and I apply it in small doses. Bill, Allie, Kelsey, and Jonathan take their meat plain and that's very good, too.

> *4 medium-size yellow onions*
> *4 cherry peppers, stemmed (I use them from a jar)*
> *3 tablespoons vegetable oil*
> *one 28-ounce can crushed tomatoes, drained*
> *one 3-pound leg of lamb, trimmed of fat and*
> *   cut into 2-inch cubes*
> *1 cup ground cumin*

1. Place the onions and cherry peppers in the bowl of a food processor and pulse to chop coarsely.

2. Heat the oil in a large skillet over medium-high heat. Add the onions and cherry peppers and cook them, stirring, until softened, about 4 minutes. Reduce the heat to low and add the tomatoes, stirring gently, until the mixture is warmed, about 2 minutes. Remove from the heat and set aside.

3. Preheat the grill.

4. Arrange the chunks of lamb on skewers, about five to a skewer. Grill them so they are slightly charred on the outside and slightly pink on the inside, about 3 to 4 minutes per side.

5. Give each person two little dishes set above their dinner plate—one dish will have cumin powder for dipping the meat and the second dish will have the tomato *sofrito* for dipping, too; or pass the mixtures in bowls if you don't have enough small dishes. Either way, it is a great combination of tastes.

COUSCOUS
À LA ELLEN

ELLEN'S TIPS

*Use whatever your
favorite herbs may be.
Some of the choices in season are dill, sweet basil,
mint, rosemary, tarragon,
or parsley.*

*Some other variations to
try are chopped almonds,
walnuts, cashews, candied
ginger, currants, grapes,
black olives, or crumbled
feta cheese.*

*To toast pine nuts, place
them on a baking sheet
and toast in a 400°F oven
until golden brown and
fragrant, 8 to 10 minutes.
Watch them.*

As much as I like to cook, I also love to find good shortcuts. I sometimes use packaged products because it is crazy not to, they can make things so easy. Instant couscous is one of those products. Once it is cooked, I doctor it up a bit with pine nuts, golden raisins, chopped cilantro leaves, and so on. Feel free to doctor your couscous with all or one of these things. Vary the herb or nut and tailor it to your likes.

> *two 10-ounce boxes couscous*
> *³/₄ cup thinly sliced scallions*
> *(white and light green parts)*
> *³/₄ cup pine nuts, lightly toasted*
> *(see Ellen's Tips)*
> *¹/₂ cup golden raisins*
> *¹/₂ cup chopped fresh cilantro leaves*
> *¹/₄ cup extra-virgin olive oil*
> *¹/₄ cup freshly squeezed lemon juice*
> *salt and freshly ground black pepper to taste*

1. Cook the couscous according to the directions on the package. Transfer the couscous to a medium-size bowl.

2. Add the scallions, pine nuts, raisins, cilantro, olive oil, and lemon juice to the couscous and toss lightly with a fork, separating the grains. Season with salt and pepper and chill for at least 1 hour before serving.

STRAWBERRY SHORTCAKES

ELLEN'S TIPS

Bake the biscuits the day before, let cool completely, and store in a cookie tin. Warm them up in a pre-heated 300°F oven for a few minutes on the day of the party just before serving.

I whip the cream without any sugar or vanilla extract because I like the taste of pure cream.

Whip the cream earlier in the day and give it another short beating just before serving. It saves time.

These are old-fashioned Strawberry Shortcakes—baking powder biscuits that are split while they are still warm, then topped with sweet strawberries and spoonfuls of fresh whipped cream. I pick up the strawberries from my farm stand in the morning, so that I can slice and sugar them early in the day, which makes them especially juicy.

This is a wonderful biscuit recipe. Remember that the less you work the dough, the more tender the biscuits will be.

2 pints fresh strawberries, washed, hulled, and thinly sliced
¹/₂ cup sugar

For the biscuits

2 cups all-purpose flour
4 teaspoons baking powder
1 teaspoon salt
1 tablespoon sugar
6 tablespoons cold vegetable shortening
³/₄ cup milk

2 cups heavy cream, whipped to stiff peaks

1. Place the strawberries in a medium-size bowl and steep them in the sugar for several hours, refrigerated.

2. Preheat the oven to 450°F.

3. Place the flour, baking powder, salt, and sugar in a large bowl. With a pastry cutter or two knives, cut the cold shortening into the dry ingredients, or use the food processor, pulsing until the dough looks like coarse meal. Add the milk and mix lightly with a fork or pulse two or three times until the dough comes together. Place the dough on a lightly floured work surface. Knead very lightly for a few turns and pat into a 1¹/₂-inch-thick piece. Cut out 3-inch rounds and place them on an ungreased cookie sheet, spaced 1 inch apart.

4. Bake until lightly brown, 10 to 12 minutes. Set aside on a wire rack to partially cool.

5. Split the biscuits open while they are still warm and spoon several tablespoons of the berries and their juice over the two halves. Place a generous dollop of whipped cream on the berries and serve.

Opposite:
STRAWBERRY SHORTCAKES

The Coolest Dinner
for the Hottest Day
of the Year

HAVARTI STICKS AND HOT AND SWEET
MUSTARD (PAGE 38)

BEST GAZPACHO

CHINESE CHICKEN SALAD

SUGAR SNAP PEAS

BROWN SUGAR PEACH PIE

Serves 6

In Bridgehampton, I usually expect the hottest day of the year to arrive some time in mid-August, although that doesn't mean it won't sneak in, and even stay for a while, in late July, or even June. Real heat makes it very still, as if life is being played out in slow motion. The breeze dies down, the sun bakes into the ground, and the heat comes up from the earth. You can see it rising. We still have weekend guests and friends over for lunch or dinner. I don't mind because there is almost always a breeze on our terrace. On the rare nights when it gets too uncomfortable to be outside, I just move everything into the kitchen where it's air-conditioned.

The hottest day of the year in Bridgehampton, though, doesn't hold a candle to an unforgettable night some years ago in Washington, D.C. Washington gets mighty humid in the summer. That night it was 89 degrees and muggy beyond belief! We had been living in Spring Valley for three years while Joe served as Deputy Secretary of the Office of Management and

Budget under the Reagan Administration. Our house had a marvelous garden, and I offered it as a place to celebrate to our Los Angeles friends in the movie industry whose granddaughter was graduating from Georgetown University. Our friends have always loved what I cook and they are very down to earth, but because of the heat I thought I would make a simple but cool meal outside by the pool. I also like to serve slices of Havarti with my hot and sweet mustard. Almost all of the meal could be prepared in advance.

It was a welcome al fresco evening. This is unquestionably the coolest dinner for the hottest night of the year—wherever that may be. Serve with a white Alsatian wine or a cold Chardonnay.

BEST GAZPACHO

ELLEN'S TIPS

*The way to keep this fresh
and crunchy is to keep
adding chopped crisp
vegetables as you serve it.
You will find that adding
a few chunks of radish,
red onion, and carrot just
before serving each time
makes a huge difference.*

*You can add more tomato
juice if you need it.*

*Taste the chili pepper to
know how hot it is. You
might want to use only a
bit of it.*

Over the years, I must have made at least twenty different gazpachos, always searching for the perfect one, which for me needs to be cool and crunchy and have a certain yin-yang balance of salty and sweet. I decided to try red onion instead of the traditional yellow in the basic recipe, and there I found the sweetness I had been looking for. The crunch comes from other untraditional ingredients: red radishes, white radishes, or jicama. Joe loves this soup and I try to keep a running supply in the fridge for him. For simple dinners on the terrace, I bring this to the table in a pitcher and serve it in chilled clear glasses. Allow enough time for it to really chill. In this case, the colder it is, the better.

6 ribs celery
1 bunch radishes, trimmed and quartered
1 medium-size red onion, quartered
1 medium-size cucumber, peeled, seeded, and cubed
2 medium-size carrots, trimmed
1 small fresh chili pepper, stemmed and seeded (optional)
6 cups tomato juice
juice of 1 lemon
1/2 cup beef broth (canned is fine)
2 tablespoons Worcestershire sauce
1 teaspoon celery salt to taste
Tabasco sauce to taste
freshly ground white pepper to taste

Trim the leafy ends from two celery ribs and place in a food processor. Set aside the other ribs. Add all the vegetables and chop them coarsely in batches in the food processor. Do not puree them. Add the tomato juice, lemon juice, beef broth, Worcestershire, and celery salt and season with Tabasco and white pepper. Taste as you go along. Chill for at least 2 hours. Serve with the remaining ribs of celery.

Best Gazpacho

CHINESE CHICKEN SALAD

ELLEN'S TIPS

Rice sticks are available at
large grocery stores in the
Asian section. You can
also find them at any
Asian grocery store.

Practice with just a few
pieces of rice noodles to
see if the oil is ready.
When the oil is the right
heat the noodle poofs
up quickly.

You can make the sauce
ahead of time. It keeps
well in a jar refrigerated.

The chicken can be baked
and shredded 1 day ahead.

Toss the salad with your
hands in a large pot or
bowl. It is much easier.

All the flavors of a traditional Chinese chicken salad—sesame oil, ginger, and scallions—come together here in a totally unique and fabulous way, on a bed of crispy, crunchy, fried rice-stick noodles and cold shredded iceberg lettuce. I can't tell you the number of times I have been asked for this recipe. If you are thinking of doubling it for your own party, do, but a word to the wise: Double everything but the chicken, which should be increased by half the original amount. If you double it outright, you will have too much chicken and not enough sauce.

For the chicken

4 whole chicken breasts (about 4 pounds),
   split into halves
2 tablespoons sesame oil
1 tablespoon soy sauce

For the salad

2 cups vegetable oil
one 5-ounce package rice sticks
3 tablespoons sesame seeds, toasted until
   golden brown (see Ellen's Tips, page 280)
6 scallions (white and green parts),
   cleaned and chopped
1 head iceberg lettuce, cored and sliced thin

For the sauce

6 tablespoons red, white, or rice wine vinegar
6 tablespoons sugar
1 tablespoon soy sauce
1 teaspoon salt
3 tablespoons sesame oil
3/4 cup vegetable or canola oil
3 tablespoons finely chopped crystallized ginger
   (see Ellen's Tips, page 280)

continued

CHINESE CHICKEN SALAD

ELLEN'S TIPS

Preheat the oven to 350°F and toast the sesame seeds on an ungreased cookie sheet until they are golden brown. You can easily use a toaster oven for this process. You can also toast them in a dry skillet over medium heat.

When you chop the crystallized ginger, you can use a food processor. It will be noisy and the result is almost like paste, but that's okay.

1. In a large glass baking dish, marinate the chicken in the sesame oil and soy sauce, turning the breasts several times, for a few hours or overnight, refrigerated.

2. Preheat the oven to 350°F. Bake the chicken in the same dish in the marinade for 25 to 30 minutes and then let cool. Remove the skin and bones and discard. Shred the chicken into bite-size pieces. Set aside until assembly time.

3. The morning of the dinner, heat the vegetable oil in a large saucepan over medium-high heat until hot but not smoking. Drop in a few rice sticks and watch them. They will poof up and turn white. Now you are ready to put in the rest of the sticks in batches. Turn the pile over and cook them on the other side. They should stay white and not turn brown. This takes only a few seconds on each side. When they stop making a sizzling noise, they are done. Drain on paper towels and set them aside until assembly.

4. In a small bowl, whisk together the sauce ingredients.

5. To assemble the salad, wait until just before eating. In a large bowl or pot, combine the chicken with the toasted sesame seeds, chopped scallions, and sliced lettuce. Pour the sauce over the salad and toss well. Place the crispy noodles on a big platter and spoon the tossed chicken salad on top of them. Serve immediately.

SUGAR SNAP PEAS

I think of sugar snap peas as lovely little treats—something special for guests at a party. Sugar snaps require almost nothing by way of cooking. Less is more, and a simple pat of softened butter brings out their best attributes. They look especially dazzling alongside the Chinese chicken salad. If you can't find sugar snaps, use tender young green beans.

1 pound sugar snap peas, trimmed
2 tablespoons butter

Clean the peas, pinch off the ends, and pull off the string, if it comes away naturally. Melt the butter in a large skillet over medium-high heat and cook the peas for a few minutes, shaking the pan constantly, until the peas turn bright green. This will take only 3 to 5 minutes. Serve immediately.

ELLEN'S TIP

You may also steam the peas if you wish. Fill a pot with about one inch of water and a bit of salt, bring to a boil, and steam the peas, preferably in a basket, for about 3 minutes. It is easy to overcook them, so be careful. I like the skillet method because it's quick and easy.

BROWN SUGAR PEACH PIE

Opposite: **BROWN SUGAR PEACH PIE**

continued

ELLEN'S TIPS

To make latticework for the top crust, roll the dough out ¼ inch thick on a lightly floured work surface. Cut the dough into ½-inch-wide strips. Place the strips, about ½ inch apart, over the pie. Fold every other strip back three fourths of its length. Lay new strips across perpendicularly to weave over and under until the lattice is complete. Even if the strip breaks, it can be patched with some water and you can continue. Make sure the lattice openings are about ½ inch in diameter. When you become more familiar with the dough, it becomes easier. Just think, if all else fails, you can roll it up in a ball, roll it out again, and make a top crust. If you overhandle the dough, however, the result may be tough. But practice makes perfect, and the next time you won't need to overhandle.

I first made this fabulous pie many years ago on Cape Cod, with my sister-in-law Joyce. At the time, Joyce didn't have a rolling pin, so I just floured up a wine bottle and used that to roll out the crust. It worked just fine. Necessity is the mother of invention. I prefer to use a rolling pin nowadays, and I'm happy to say that the pie remains in my file. The peaches come from the orchard right down the road. Wherever you get your peaches, be sure that they are ripe.

I've provided directions for making both a double-crust and lattice-top pie. I must admit that the lattice top is more work but worth it. If you've never made one, don't give up before you start. Lattice tops are easier than you think. Just follow the directions, strip by strip.

MAKES ONE 9-INCH PIE

6 to 8 large ripe peaches, peeled and sliced
1 tablespoon all-purpose flour, plus extra for assembling the pie
¼ teaspoon ground cinnamon
¼ teaspoon freshly grated nutmeg
1 tablespoon freshly squeezed lemon juice
1 tablespoon freshly grated lemon zest
2 recipes Foolproof Pie Crust (page 284)
½ cup firmly packed brown sugar (light or dark)
½ cup sour cream
2 tablespoons unsalted butter, cut into small pieces

1. Preheat the oven to 400°F.

2. Peel and pit the peaches, then slice them into a large bowl. Add the 1 tablespoon flour, the cinnamon, nutmeg, lemon juice, and zest to the bowl and toss the peaches to distribute the mixture evenly. Set aside.

3. Roll out half the pie crust dough, ¼ inch thick, onto a lightly floured work surface, and fit it into a 9-inch pie plate. Put in half the peaches. Sprinkle with half the brown sugar and add 3 or 4 dollops of the sour cream. Layer in the rest of the peaches and the rest of the brown sugar and sour cream, finishing with the pieces of butter.

4. Roll out the top crust ¼ inch thick and place it over the peaches. With a sharp knife, cut around the pie plate at the edge to make a perfect circle. Take a fork, dip the tines into some flour, and press around the two crusts to join them. Make six or seven 1-inch-long vents in the crust to allow the steam to escape.

continued

Peeling peaches is a cinch. Boil a pot of water. Drop them one at a time into the water for 30 seconds, then remove with a slotted spoon. Working under cold running water (so your fingers don't burn), peel the skin off. Make sure peaches are ripe for easy peeling.

To make rolling the dough easier, flour your rolling pin and work surface. Don't be afraid to gently pick up the dough and turn it to prevent it from sticking.

To transfer the dough to the pie plate, loosely roll the dough around your rolling pin and unwrap it over the pie plate. This prevents the dough from tearing.

If you are using a food processor to prepare the dough, pulse on and off until the mixture resembles coarse meal. When the milk is added the dough will form a ball. Stop pulsing at this point so the dough isn't overworked.

Slip a cookie sheet under the pie while it is baking to prevent the bubbling pie juices from making a mess of the oven.

5. Bake the pie in the center of the oven for 10 minutes, reduce the oven temperature to 350°F, and bake until the crust is brown and the peaches are bubbling, 35 to 40 minutes.

FOOLPROOF PIE CRUST

In 1959, when I was living in Berkeley, California, for the summer, a pretty German girl lived next door. She was always cooking wonderful things and I especially liked her pies. She gave me this recipe, assuring me that it was foolproof. She was right! I have used it ever since and still find it to be among the best crusts I've ever tried. It also bakes up into the most delicious cookies. They are so good, in fact, that when they are made, they are usually gone in one night, so I double the recipe.

MAKES ONE 9-INCH CRUST

1¼ cups all-purpose flour, plus extra for dusting
1 teaspoon baking powder
2 tablespoons granulated sugar
pinch of salt
½ cup vegetable shortening
¼ cup milk

Sift the flour, baking powder, sugar, and salt together in a medium-size bowl. Cut in the shortening with a pastry blender or two knives until the mixture resembles coarse meal. You may also use a food processor (see Ellen's Tips). Add the milk, little by little, working with a fork until the mixture comes together. Turn the dough onto a lightly floured work surface and roll it out so it is about ¼ inch thick. Do not overhandle the dough. Transfer it to a 9-inch pie plate for your pie. Or form it into a ball, wrap in plastic, and refrigerate for up to 3 days.

VARIATION

We love Pie Crust Cookies in our house. To make this recipe, roll out the dough to ¼-inch thickness and sprinkle it heavily with a mixture of cinnamon and sugar (⅔ cup sugar and 1 teaspoon ground cinnamon). With a sharp knife, cut into 3-inch squares and place on an ungreased cookie sheet. Bake at 425°F until the cookies are lightly browned, 10 to 12 minutes. This will make about 30 cookies.

INDEX

De Combray, Richard, 142
Delaney, Rose, 258
desserts:
    apricot sherbet, 165
    Aunt Sadye's brownies, 201
    homemade vanilla ice cream, 26
    lace cookies, 166
    Mexican flan with raspberries, 234
    persimmon pudding with hard sauce, 58–59
    pumpkin swirl cheesecake, 42–44
    rhubarb and yogurt parfaits, 136
    see also cakes; pies, dessert
deviled eggs for a nosh, 159
dill:
    in mom's marinated cucumbers, 218
    in salmon mousse, 142–44
    sauce, poached salmon with, 252–54
    tips on, 218
dips:
    curry, 181
    yogurt and blue cheese, 193
    yogurt and blue cheese, crudités with, 192–93
Donahoe, Anne, chocolate roll of, 110–12
Donahoe, Daniel, 110
dressings:
    blue cheese, iceberg wedges with, 163
    Ellen's, *see* Ellen's dressing
dumplings:
    parsleyed, chicken fricassee with, 133–34
    stewed tomatoes with, 162

eggs:
    crumbled, asparagus with, 148
    deviled, for a nosh, 159
    hard-boiled, in Meredith's caviar pie, 104
    hard-boiled, tips for, 159
Ellen's dressing:
    in asparagus with crumbled eggs, 148
    big green salad with, 231–32
    butter lettuce salad with, 135
    in Caesar salad, 242

    version I of, 232–33
    version II of, 232–33
    watercress salad with, 76
enchiladas verdes, chicken, 230–31
endive:
    in big green salad with Ellen's dressing, 232–33
    and Mandarin orange salad, 200
    in mixed greens with cherry tomatoes, 90
    spinach, and watercress salad, 185
    and watercress salad with Ellen's dressing, 76
entertaining, rules of, xxiii–xxiv

Farmer cheese, in Russian blintzes with sour cream and black cherry preserves, 78–79
figs, in savory toasts, 250
"finger test," for doneness of meat, 194
fish:
    poached salmon with dill sauce, 252–54
    salmon mousse, 142–44
    swordfish my way, 216
    tips on, 216
flan, Mexican, with raspberries, 234
flour, seasoned, 18
flower arrangements, xxv
foolproof pie crust, 284
Fourth of July, 206, 249–59
French-style dishes:
    asparagus quiche, 171, 174
    beef bourguignonne, 85–88
Friday Harbor apple pie, 24–25
frosting:
    chocolate, 153
    cream cheese, 121
    mocha, 177

Gardens, xix, 125, 206
garlic bread, 241
gazpacho, best, 276
Gazzara, Ben, 238
Gilbert, Sally, 189

M&M's, chocolate cloud cake with, 243–45

margaritas, Bob's, 222

mashed potatoes, 39

   gravy for, 40

meat loaf, old-fashioned, 36

Meredith's caviar pie, 104

Mexican recipes, 221–34

   Bob's margaritas, 222

   chicken enchiladas verdes, 230–31

   flan with raspberries, 234

   guacamole, 226

   tortilla soup, 227–29

mint, fresh, sauce, leg of lamb with, and roasted potatoes, 106–7

Mitch (author's ex-husband), 158

mix-and-match rule for entertaining, xxiv

mocha frosting, 177

mom's marinated cucumbers, 218

Monterey Jack cheese:

   in Chicago corn pudding, 219

   in chicken enchiladas verdes, 230–31

   in short-circuit corn bread, 188

   in tortilla soup, 227–29

Moroccan-style dishes:

   in couscous à la Ellen, 268

   shish kebabs, 267

mousse, salmon, 142–44

mozzarella cheese, in tomato phyllo pizza, 130

mud pie, 14–15

mustard, hot and sweet, 38

mustard greens, 118–19

Myles (author's brother), 4, 16

my stack, 32

New Year's Eve, 64, 103–12

New York's finest chicken salad, 237

Nicolayevsky, Claudia, 234

noodles, buttered, 99

nutmeg, fresh, angel food cake with sliced pears, crème anglaise and, 91–93

Old-fashioned meat loaf, 36

olives:

   in savory toasts, 250

   in sesame short ribs with tortillas, 18–19

onion puffs, 68

orange:

   -cranberry relish, 56

   Mandarin, and endive salad, 200

orange juice, hint on squeezing of, 32

Oreo cookies, in mud pie, 14–15

Pancakes:

   my stack, 32

   Russian blintzes with sour cream and black cherry preserves, 78–79

   Southern Hill's stack, 31

   tips on, 32

pan-grilled veal chops, 10

panic, avoidance of, in entertaining, xxiii–xxiv

paprika:

   in cheese straws, 17

   in chicken paprikash, 97

   kinds of, 97

parfaits, rhubarb and yogurt, 136

Parmesan cheese:

   in Caesar salad, 242

   in potato pie South African style, 196–97

   in stuffed shells with red sauce, 238–40

parsleyed:

   dumplings, chicken fricassee with, 133–34

   green beans, 22

pasta, stuffed shells with red sauce, 238–40

pâté, chicken liver, with cornichons, 169–70

pea(s):

   and lima bean puree, 11

   split, soup, Mama's, 71–72

   sugar snap, 281

   sweet garden, 57

peach(es):

   peeling of, 284

   pie, brown sugar, 282–84

Rose's blueberry pie, 258–59
Russian blintzes with sour cream and black
    cherry preserves, 78–79
Rydell, Mark, xiii

Salads:
    big green, with Ellen's dressing, 232–33
    butter lettuce, 135
    Caesar, 242
    Chinese chicken, 278–80
    endive and Mandarin orange, 200
    iceberg wedges with blue cheese dressing, 163
    mixed greens with cherry tomatoes, 90
    mom's marinated cucumbers, 218
    New York's finest chicken, 237
    spinach, endive, and watercress, 185
    watercress, with Ellen's dressing, 76
Sally's crunchy almond cheesecake, 189–90
salmon:
    mousse, 142–44
    poached, with dill sauce, 252–54
saltines, White House, 215
sauces:
    dill, poached salmon with, 252–54
    fresh mint, leg of lamb with, and roasted
        potatoes, 106–7
    gravy, for mashed potatoes, 40
    green tomatillo, for chicken enchiladas verdes,
        230–31
    hard, persimmon pudding with, 58–59
    hot fudge, 112
    pineapple, tomato aspic with, 175
    red, stuffed shells with, 238–40
sautéed zucchini, 41
savory toasts, 250
sesame (seeds):
    in Chinese chicken salad, 278–80
    short ribs with tortillas, 18–19
    toasting of, 280
    wafers, 8
shells, stuffed, with red sauce, 238–40

sherbet, apricot, 165
shish kebabs, Moroccan-style, 267
shortcakes, strawberry, 270
short ribs, sesame, with tortillas, 18–19
simplicity rule for entertaining, xxiii
sorrel soup, 263–64
soup:
    best gazpacho, 276
    Mama's split pea, 71–72
    sorrel, 263–64
    tomato carrot, 212
    tortilla, 227–29
sour cream:
    in Chicago corn pudding, 219
    in chicken paprikash, 97
    in cold berry pie, 220
    curdled, 97
    in curry dip, 181
    in Meredith's caviar pie, 104
    Russian blintzes with black cherry preserves
        and, 78–79
    in Sally's crunchy almond cheesecake, 189–90
South African style potato pie, 196–97
Southern Hill's stack, 31
spinach:
    endive, and watercress salad, 185
    steamed, 257
split pea soup, Mama's, 71–72
sponge cake, chocolate, 176–77
steak, Lillian's baked, 194
steamed spinach, 257
stewed tomatoes with dumplings, 162
stews:
    beef bourguignonne, 85–88
    chicken fricassee with parsleyed dumplings,
        133–34
    lamb shanks with white beans, 116
strawberry shortcakes, 270
stuffed shells with red sauce, 238–40
stuffing, bread, roast turkey with, 48, 51
sugar snap peas, 281
sunflower seeds and yams, 52–53

Susan's bourbon cake, 101–2
sweet-and-sour red cabbage, 100
swordfish my way, 216

Tennis playing, 221
tequila, in Bob's margaritas, 222
Thanksgiving, 4, 45–59
Theresa (author's daughter's friend), 119, 243
toasts, savory, 250
tomatillos, in chicken enchiladas verdes, 230–31
tomato(es):
    aspic with pineapple sauce, 175
    broiled, 13
    carrot soup, 212
    cherry, in big green salad with Ellen's dressing,
        232–33
    cherry, mixed greens with, 90
    in lamb shanks with white beans, 116
    in Moroccan-style shish kebabs, 267
    phyllo pizza, 130
    stewed, with dumplings, 162
    in tortilla soup, 227–29
tomato juice:
    in best gazpacho, 276
    in tomato carrot soup, 212
tortilla(s):
    in chicken enchiladas verdes, 230–31
    sesame short ribs with, 18–19
    soup, 227–29
turkey with bread stuffing, roast, 48, 51

Valentine's Day, 113–21
vanilla:
    in crème anglaise, 93
    ice cream, homemade, 26
    pudding, in golden bundt cake with chocolate
        leaves, 150–54
veal:
    chops, pan-grilled, 10
    in old-fashioned meat loaf, 36

vegetables, hint on cooking of, 22
vermicelli, in Kevin's pilaf, 89

Wafers, sesame, 8
walnuts:
    in Aunt Sadye's brownies, 201
    in persimmon pudding with hard sauce, 58–59
watercress:
    salad, with Ellen's dressing, 76
    spinach, and endive salad, 185
white beans, lamb shanks with, 116
White House saltines, 215
Wilson, Stella, 153, 196
wine, red, in lamb shanks with white beans, 116
Wright, Ann, 71, 96, 97, 175
Wright, David, 64, 83, 110, 206
Wright, Ellen (author):
    culinary background of, xix–xx
    family background of, xix, 24, 64, 145
Wright, Joe (author's father-in-law), 96
Wright, Joe (Bobby) (author's husband), xviii,
        xx, 63, 71, 158, 249
    family background of, 96
    garden of, xix, 125
    on New Year's Eve, 64, 103
    in Reagan administration, 274–75
    tennis playing of, 221
Wright, Tiffany, 206

Yams and sunflower seeds, 52–53
yogurt:
    and blue cheese dip, crudités with, 192–93
    and blue cheese dip, recipe for, 193
    and rhubarb parfaits, 136
Yorkshire pudding:
    recipe for, 147
    roast beef with, 145–47

Zucchini, sautéed, 41